The Shape of the Puritan Mind

The Shape of the Puritan Mind

THE THOUGHT OF SAMUEL WILLARD

Ernest Benson Lowrie

YALE UNIVERSITY PRESS
NEW HAVEN AND LONDON
1974

*Published with assistance from the
foundation established in memory
of Philip Hamilton McMillan of
the Class of 1894, Yale College.*

*Library of Congress catalog card number: 74–76650
International standard book number: 0–300–01714–6*

*Designed by Sally Sullivan
and set in Baskerville type.
Printed in the United States of America by
The Colonial Press Inc., Clinton, Mass.*

*Published in Great Britain, Europe, and Africa by
Yale University Press, Ltd., London.
Distributed in Latin America by Kaiman & Polon,
Inc., New York City; in Australasia and Southeast
Asia by John Wiley & Sons Australasia Pty. Ltd.,
Sydney; in India by UBS Publishers' Distributors Pvt.,
Ltd., Delhi; in Japan by John Weatherhill, Inc., Tokyo.*

For Joyce and Michele

Samuel Willard . . . was absolute master of the vast body of Protestant learning, of that compendium of physics, mathematics, logic, rhetoric which had constituted the European intellect at the time of the Great Migration. . . . *A Compleat Body of Divinity* [is] a landmark in American publishing and a magnificent summation of the Puritan intellect.

Perry Miller

Contents

Acknowledgments

Scholars too numerous to mention have enriched my understanding of the Puritan movement in Colonial New England. A few teachers, however, stand out because of their decisive contribution to my interpretation of the thought of Samuel Willard. Edmund S. Morgan introduced me to Puritan studies, Sydney E. Ahlstrom nurtured my interest in American religious thought, Robert L. Calhoun exposed me to the development of Christian doctrine, George A. Lindbeck guided me through late medieval and early modern thought, and Julian N. Hartt taught me more than academic theology.

My deepest gratitude is expressed to my students, my wife Joyce, and my daughter Michele. They formed the audience for whom this study was written.

Introduction

> *The vast majority of the colonial people, said Robert Baird, "were simply Christians, who knew of no way by which men can be good or happy but that pointed out by God in his Word." By just such emphasis on the simple Christianity of the colonial churches, Baird was serving as accomplice to what might almost be called a conspiracy to obliterate the original dedication to a highly intellectual system of theology, a project in which, by the way, the historian Bancroft and the romancer Cooper joined. The great achievements of the provincial mind before the Revolutionary agitation were in systematic theology.*
>
> Perry Miller[1]

The distinctive breed of Englishmen who staked out their claim on the Massachusetts Bay in the 1630s arrived with more than meager materials and willing hands. They also had some ideas, for they were Puritans, or even more technically put, they were advocates of a certain type of Puritanism now known by the rather awkward title, "Non-Separating Congregationalism." [2] Included in their midst

1. Perry Miller, *The Life of the Mind in America: From the Revolution to the Civil War* (New York, 1965), p. 69.
2. See Perry Miller, *Orthodoxy in Massachusetts: 1630–1650* (Cambridge, Mass., 1933).

were a large number of university men who were much
given to argument and ordered reflection on the ultimate
questions. Having the courage of their convictions and a
splendid opportunity to practice what they preached, they
infused their errand into the wilderness of North America
with a comprehensive and meticulously formulated body
of beliefs to shape the new society's self-understanding and
action. Churches and schools were established to guarantee
that their children were well instructed in the faith. One
of their star protégés was Samuel Willard (1640–1707).
Born at the end of "the Great Migration," reared on the
frontier, and educated at Harvard College, Willard later
emerged as the teacher of the Old South Church of Boston,
and during the last six years of his life, the acting president
of Harvard. In season and out Willard carried on the theological enterprise, expounding the faith to the faithful, de-
fending it from its adversaries, and re-examining it in the
light of the new situation of Massachusetts during the pain-
ful transition from colony to province. Although his thought
exhibits the depth and breadth of the cultural heritage
New England received from England and the medieval
universities, his lived experience and education were in-
clusively American. To grasp the substantive core of his
thought is to gain access to the initial stage of the life of
the mind as it developed in the soil and soul of America.

Samuel Willard arrests the attention of the student of the
Puritan adventure in seventeenth-century Massachusetts by
the comprehensive character of his published works. Among
the numerous theologians who graced the colonial period of
American history, he holds the distinction of being the one
who wrote the most thoroughly and systematically on "the
whole circle of religion." Admittedly, others surpassed him
in originality and profundity. Some even managed to flesh
out a few particular points in the Puritan creed more fully
than he. Yet Willard's lifework in systematic theology stands
unequalled in scope until after the Revolution. If the testi-

mony of Thomas Prince and Joseph Sewall is to be credited, "many of the most knowing and judicious persons both from town and college" were yearning for the posthumous publication of Willard's two hundred fifty expository lectures on the Westminster Shorter Catechism which they edited and introduced with the fitting title, *A Compleat Body of Divinity* (1726). In their opinion, the interest in these lectures had "strangely rather increased than declined for these eighteen years" since Willard's death: "hardly any book has been more passionately wished for" than this massive tome, so enormous that the presses of Boston had to pool their resources in printing its nearly one thousand double-columned folio pages. Roughly one and a half times as long as John Calvin's *Institutes of the Christian Religion*, it is the closest thing to being a *Summa Theologiae* that Puritan New England ever produced.[3]

A Compleat Body of Divinity, moreover, was only one of no less than fifty separate works Willard wrote, or perhaps one should say spoke, for virtually all his publications were derived from public lectures or sermons. Some, of course, were brief pieces but more than a few were extended discourses on recondite doctrines or detailed considerations of difficult passages from the Bible. Together they form an impressive monument to the Puritans' thirst for sermons "to lead them up some higher pinnacle of thought, or pile upon their sturdy minds some heavier weight of argument."[4]

3. "Preface" to CB. On p. 666 an editorial note states: "The reader is desired to observe, that by reason of several presses, being made use of in this large work, it has fallen out (as is frequent in such cases) that the pages for a considerable way, are numbered over again." Because there are two sets of numbers from 581 to 666, the second series is indicated in notes with an asterisk.

4. Horace Bushnell, "The Age of Homespun," *Work and Play: or Literary Varieties* (New York, 1864), pp. 387ff. Quoted by Sydney E. Ahlstrom, "Theology in America: A Historical Survey," *The Shaping of American Religion*, ed. James Ward Smith and A. Leland Jamison (Princeton, N.J., 1961), p. 233.

Arguments Willard held in plenty, and nothing that exercised the imagination and mind of a typical Puritan intellectual escaped Willard's comment. When careful scholars
of particular facets in colonial New England's life and
thought set out to register the central, mainline tradition,
Willard has a fitting quotation readily available. For example, in *The Puritan Family* Edmund S. Morgan cites
Willard five times in the first three pages in order to es-
tablish the representative position. And Morgan begins his
article, "Puritans and Sex," in which he attempts to show
that the Puritans were not responsible for Victorian
"squeamishness" on sexual matters, with this observation:

> At the outset, consider the Puritans' attitude toward mar-
> riage and the role of sex in marriage. The popular assump-
> tion might be that the Puritans frowned on marriage and
> tried to hush up the physical aspect of it as much as possi-
> ble, but listen to what they themselves had to say. Samuel
> Willard, minister of the Old South Church in the latter part
> of the seventeenth century and author of the most complete
> textbook of Puritan Divinity, more than once expressed his
> horror at "that popish conceit of the excellency of virgin-
> ity." [5]

The opening sentence in chapter one of Alan Ludwig's
masterful study of Puritan iconography, *Graven Images*,
reads: "Samuel Willard . . . had a great deal to say about
how language should function in investigating man's knowledge of God." And Willard's theories clearly shape Ludwig's
entire initial section, "The Function of Symbolism in Normative Puritan Theology." [6] *The Character of the Good
Ruler* by T. H. Breen takes its title directly from Willard's
1694 election sermon, which is reproduced on the frontis-

5. Edmund S. Morgan, *The Puritan Family* (Boston, 1956), pp. 9–11;
"The Puritans and Sex," *New England Quarterly* (Dec., 1942), p. 591.
6. Alan Ludwig, *Graven Images* (Middletown, Conn., 1966), pp.
21–32.

piece.[7] Willard's centrality in the Puritan movement as it achieved institutional maturity is registered most powerfully, however, by the sheer weight given to him in Perry Miller's seminal volume, *The New England Mind: The Seventeenth Century*. About one of ten original references are to Willard, and in one chapter the ratio rises to slightly more than one of four.[8]

Moses Coit Tyler was the one man during the nineteenth century whose opinion on Willard was informed by extensive scholarship in the colonial period. His extended comments on Willard's magnum opus are worth quoting in full:

> "A Complete Body of Divinity" is a vast book, in all senses; by no one to be trifled with. Let us salute it with uncovered heads.
>
> The thought and expression of this literary mammoth are lucid, firm, close. The author moves over the great spaces of his subject with a calm and commanding tread, as one well assured both of himself and of the ground he walked on. His object seemed to be, not merely to enlighten the mind, but to elevate the character and the life; and whenever, in the discussion of a topic, he has finished the merely logical process, he advances at once to the practical bearings of it, and urges upon his hearers the deductions of a moral logic, always doing this earnestly, persuasively, and in a kingly way. The whole effect is nutritious to brain and to moral sense; and the book might still serve to make men good Christians as well as good theologians—if only there were still left upon the earth the men capable of reading it.[9]

7. T. H. Breen, *The Character of the Good Ruler* (New Haven, Conn., 1970).

8. Miller's notes unfortunately were not published with the text (New York, 1939); the original documentation is available in the Houghton Library of Harvard University.

9. Moses Coit Tyler, *A History of American Literature, 1607-1765* (New York, 1962), with a new foreword by Perry Miller, pp. 403-404; the original edition was published in 1878.

A careful reading of Willard's "Systematical Divinity" is the primary intention of this study. The analytic task of unpacking his technical language is balanced by the synthesizing task of showing the play of various distinctions and concepts in the fabric of his thought. Broadly speaking, the exposition moves from Willard's metaphysical beliefs to his ethical theory, to his Christian reflections on the human situation in the light of the cardinal mysteries of the Puritan creed.

No attempt is made to trace the various ideas to their origins. Neither is it the intent to seize upon one or two organizing motifs to differentiate Willard's theology from other positions. While it would be quite easy to state that on this or that point Willard disagrees with John Calvin, or follows the Augustinian tradition, or sides with Duns Scotus against Thomas Aquinas, the temptation to do so is resisted, for not only would it increase the size of this volume considerably, but more important, it would also upset the proportion and progression of the exposition.

While the main purpose is to explicate straightforwardly the substantive content of Willard's thought, this study is also intended as a guide to the mentality of Puritan America, for the entire movement shared a rich common language and mode of thought. Without downgrading the intensity and range of controversy among the quarrelsome colonists, expressed in their vast polemical literature, one should not be blind to the overarching agreement that remains on their central concerns. Indeed, when Philip Schaff delivered his inaugural address at Mercersburg Theological Seminary in 1844, this trained observer and expert in church history from the most advanced centers of learning in Germany simply asserted the obvious when he claimed that "the reigning theology of the country . . . is the theology of the Westminster Confession." For all their disagreements over "distinctives," different denominations and antagonistic camps within the denominations, when "viewed as a whole," could still be gathered under the broad seventeenth-century tent of Westminster.[10] In *A Religious History of the American People,* Sydney E. Ahlstrom makes a similar claim:

> . . . these Westminster standards constitute one of the classic formulations of Reformed theology. That so many learned and contentious men in an age of so much theological hair-splitting could with so little coercion establish so resounding a consensus on so detailed a doctrinal statement is one of the marvels of the century. Nor were these formulations forgotten amid wars and violence; they remain normative in Scotland and their immense influence on the thought and practice of American Congregationalists, Presbyterians, and Baptists makes them by far the most important confessional witness in American colonial history. Insusceptible to easy or brief summary, they and the derivative confessions deserve close attention from any student of early American Protestantism.[11]

These specialists in American theology are as sensitive to the deviations as to the continuities in competing positions, for their nuances are the stuff of history. The point being made here, however, is that well into the nineteenth century most American Protestants still conceived of "Orthodoxy" as being the Westminster Confession. Because Westminster occupied the ground floor of theology in America, rebels as well as reactionaries assumed familiarity with its substantive content. For good or ill it simply is the case that in order to achieve an adequate grasp of the historical foundations of American culture one must penetrate the inner workings of the Puritan mind, for it commanded the

10. Philip Schaff, *The Principle of Protestantism as Related to the Present State of the Church* (Chambersburg, Pa., 1845), p. 114.

11. Sydney E. Ahlstrom, *A Religious History of the American People* (New Haven, Conn., 1972), p. 94; see also, p. 453.

massive center of the colonial period. No American ever
expounded the ancient creed more thoroughly than that
"Teacher of a Church in Boston," [12] Samuel Willard.

12. This is the most frequent identification given after Willard's
name on the title pages of his books.

CHAPTER ONE

Teacher of a Church in Boston

*In him [Samuel Willard] bountiful heaven was
pleased to cause a concurrence of all those natural and
acquired, moral and spiritual excellencies, which are
necessary to constitute a great man, a profound divine,
a very considerable scholar, and an heavenly Christian.
In the light and influence of these perfections, he appeared as a star of the first magnitude in the orb of the
church.*

*The God of Nature was pleased with a liberal hand
to bestow on him those natural intellectual endowments, which laid the foundation of great improvement in knowledge. And did from his youth presage
uncommon service for God and his people, which his
Master had designed him for. In natural endowments,
he appeared as the elder son among many brethren.
In these very few, if any, could pretend to stand upon
a level with him. The natural capacity of his soul was
of that distinction, that it seemed an undeniable con-
futation of the doctrine of the equality of souls; and
left it no longer problematical.*

Ebenezer Pemberton[1]

1. Ebenezer Pemberton, *A Funeral Sermon on the Death of that
Learned and Excellent Divine, the Reverend Mr. Samuel Willard*
(Boston, Mass., 1707), pp. 60–63. For a full biographical statement, see
Seymour Van Dyken, *Samuel Willard, 1640–1707: Preacher of Orthodoxy in an Era of Change* (Grand Rapids, Mich., 1972), especially the
first five chapters. (In quotations throughout the present work, spelling,
punctuation, and capitalization have been modernized.)

Before his matriculation at Harvard College during the summer of 1655, nothing in Samuel Willard's life can be documented except for the solitary fact that he was born in Concord, Massachusetts on 31 January, 1640, the sixth child of Simon and Mary Willard.[2]

Simon Willard (1605–76) landed in New England as a man of twenty-nine at the height of the Puritan migration to the Massachusetts Bay Colony. Initially settling in Cambridge (then called Newtown), he and the Reverend Peter Bulkeley soon moved to the frontier and founded Concord during 1635 and 1636. Simon was Concord's Deputy to the General Court from 1635 to 1654 (with the exception of the years 1643, 1647, and 1648). Furthermore, he was actively engaged in military affairs. After serving as the "surveyor of arms" in Concord for a decade, Simon advanced to the rank of captain, and then in 1653 he was elected major by Middlesex County. Except for a brief period when he was temporarily elevated to "commander in chief of the United Colonies," Simon remained a major till his death during King Philip's War in 1676.

Simon Willard's adventures along the frontier, bargaining with the Indians or laying out a new town line, surely fired the imagination of young Samuel.[3] Many an evening must Samuel have overheard conversations with the local minister, the Reverend Peter Bulkeley, in which everything, from political intrigue to the minutiae of theology, was covered.

Peter Bulkeley (1583–1659) was one of the abler ministers to immigrate to Massachusetts with a Cambridge University

2. Joseph Willard, *Willard Memoir; or, Life and Times of Major Simon Willard* (Boston, Mass., 1858), p. 357.

3. Ibid., pp. 129, 132, 135–39, 140–48, 154, 188, 193–283. See also *Records of the Governor and Company of the Massachusetts Bay in New England*, 1: 191, 221, 323; 2: 117; 3: 62, 359; 4, part 1: 98f., 109, 217. Simon Willard's most famous adventure was discovering the northern boundary of the colony, when he determined that the "most northerly part of the Merrimack River" was 43°40′12″ in latitude.

degree (M.A. 1608). His major publication, *The Gospel Covenant: or, the Covenant of Grace Opened* (1641), is considered by Perry Miller "the outstanding work" written on this central doctrine by a first-generation American Puritan.[4] Not only was Samuel exposed to his weekly sermons; in all probability Peter Bulkeley prepared him academically for entrance to Harvard College.[5]

History is silent on any decisive turning points during Samuel Willard's early years. Perhaps a diary will someday be found that relates his experiences of conviction, conversion, and calling to the ministry. All that the record reveals is that during his fifteenth year Samuel entered Harvard College shortly after "The Laws of the College" were updated and codified in 1655. Four years in President Charles Chauncy's "School of the Prophets" earned him a bachelor of arts degree in 1659. Although Willard remained at the college for advanced theological studies, he failed, for reasons that still puzzle Harvard antiquarians, to receive the master's degree in 1662.[6] The only personal note we

4. Perry Miller, *The New England Mind: The Seventeenth Century* (Cambridge, Mass., 1954), p. 504.

5. Charles H. Walcott, *Concord in the Colonial Period* (Boston, Mass., 1884), pp. 128–29: ". . . it is said, that there was a grammar school in Concord before 1680; but, in the earlier years of the settlement, there could have been no regular instruction of the youth, except what was supplied by the minister and by parents; and it is not likely that there was any school-house, or building specially devoted to school purposes, at any time preceding the gift of Captain Timothy Wheeler, in 1687."

6. George Lyman Kittredge, "A Harvard Salutatory Oration of 1662," *Publications of the Colonial Society*, 28 (1935), n. 14: "Samuel Willard (A.B. 1659) received a Master's degree at some time. If the ordinary term of three years only had elapsed, his A.M. would have been granted in 1662. In the Triennial of 1674 Willard's name occurs without the A.M.; so also in that of 1682; but in the Triennial of 1698 he appears as 'Samuel Willard Mr. Socius.' It is clear, then, that Willard received his A.M. out of course, in some year after 1674 but before or in 1698. Thus the year 1662 remains Masterless. Mr. Albert Matthews has helped me here by excluding Willard from 1662." It should be noted that the M.A. appears after Willard's name on the title pages of his books only in posthumous editions.

have about Willard's career as a Harvard student is that he
frequently paid his "quarter-bills" in kind, one October
with "17 quarts of hot waters at 2s per quart." [7]

In 1663 Samuel Willard sealed a solemn covenant with
the town of Groton, a new frontier settlement, in which
it was agreed that he would be "their minister as long as
he lives . . . except a manifest providence of God appears
to take him off." [8] A year later he married Abigail, the
sixteen-year-old daughter of the Reverend John Sherman of
Watertown, who bore him six children.[9]

What occasioned Willard's first publication was the
bizarre behavior of a frenzied young girl, Elizabeth Knap,
In the preface to *Useful Instructions* (1673), Willard as-
sured the congregation and world that he had "not en-
deavored to varnish or paint" over the sordid details. And
his manuscript, "A brief account of a strange and unusual
providence of God, befallen to Elizabeth Knap of Groton,"
remains as one of the most insightful documents on witchcraft and demon possession from the period.[10]

When Elizabeth pointed an accusing finger at a neighbor
as the one tormenting her, Willard moved instantly to cur-
tail the "raising of spirits against such as we are ready to
think may be his [Satan's] subservient actors in this case."
In Willard's sermon to the agitated town he declared forth-
rightly that to follow that course "is the way to provocation

7. Samuel Eliot Morison, *Harvard in the Seventeenth Century* (Cambridge, Mass., 1936), p. 104. See John Langdon Sibley, *Graduates of
Harvard College*, 1: 573; 2: 13–36.
8. Samuel A. Green, M.D., ed., *The Early Records of Groton, Massachusetts, 1662–1707* (Groton, Mass., 1880), p. 8.
9. Henry Bond, *Family Memorial* (Boston, Mass., 1855), p. 432.
10. Published in *Collections of the Massachusetts Historical Society*,
4th ser., 8: pp. 555–70. It can also be found in Samuel A. Green, M.D.,
Groton in the Witchcraft Times (Groton, Mass., 1883). Green's claim
that Willard sent the manuscript to Cotton Mather (p. 5) is obviously
a mistake; it was sent to Increase Mather. For a recent discussion of the
case, see Chadwick Hansen, *Witchcraft at Salem* (New York, 1969), pp.
38–42.

and exasperation, to bitterness and rage." His finale would be trite were the situation less volatile. But "when God thus leaves the common track, and comes in so unwonted a way of judgment," it is best for ministers to follow the familiar paths—"Let us lay aside envy and malice, throw down our contention and strife, and take up peace and love." [11] While Willard's ministrations seemed to have little impact upon Elizabeth, he did keep Groton from becoming a horrid precursor to Salem.[12]

Willard's exit from Groton, however, was traumatic, for on 13 March, 1676, some four hundred Indians led by "one eyed John" set the torch to the town. Of seventy-two dwellings only six fortified garrisons remained standing.[13] With apocalyptic overtones Increase Mather pronounced that Groton's "candlestick was removed out of its place," [14] but soon a more providential rendering of King Philip's War emerged. God had a hand in it, Ebenezer Pemberton

11. UI, pp. 31, 43. See Publications by Samuel Willard (p. 239) for key to his works.

12. In 1662 one Ann Cole in Hartford managed to implicate a neighbor who was executed; see Cotton Mather, *Magnalia Christi Americana* (London, 1702), 6, vii, p. 67. When Perry Miller asserts that if Willard's "clinical report" on Elizabeth Knap "had been studied [it] might have cured the Salem wenches," he claims too much, for there are no indications that Willard cured Elizabeth in the least. Prayer and cross-examination were the only procedures Willard employed against the demonic. *The New England Mind: From Colony to Province* (Cambridge, Mass., 1953), p. 205. And Clifford K. Shipton is overly generous in his claim, "No modern report of psychic phenomena is more acutely critical and levelheaded than that sent Increase Mather by the Reverend Samuel Willard of Groton," in "The New England Clergy of the 'Glacial Age'," *Publication of the Colonial Society of Massachusetts,* 32 (1937): 40. The picture that does emerge, however, stands in striking contrast to the popular image of the clergy's role in the witchcraft episode during the last decade of the seventeenth century.

13. Samuel A. Green, M.D., *Groton During the Indian Wars* (Groton, Mass., 1883), especially pp. 7–8, 28–43.

14. Increase Mather, *A Brief History of the War with the Indians in New-England* (London, 1676), p. 24. Willard did not write a deliverance narrative.

informed the Old South Church of Boston in his funeral
oration for Samuel Willard thirty-one years later.

> The providence that occasioned his [Willard's] removal to
> this place [Boston] was an awful judgment upon the whole
> land; yet was eventually a mercy in this respect, that it made
> way for the translation of this bright star to a more con-
> spicuous orb; where his influence was more extensive and
> beneficial; and in this it was a great blessing to this congre-
> gation, to this town, nay, to all New-England.[15]

To the desolate flock making its way to neighboring towns
in 1676 the "great blessing" remained hidden, but the event
was manifest enough. King Philip's War released Willard
from his covenant with Groton and opened the way for
this thirty-six-year-old minister from the hinterland to become a luminary in Boston society. The disaster that befell
Groton was the fulcrum on which Willard's life rose from
obscurity to eminence.

The world Willard entered after 1676 was significantly
different from that of his childhood, youth, and early man-
hood. The first generation had passed from the historical
stage and now the responsibility for conducting and shaping the affairs of the Bay Colony devolved upon the
descendants. The task of this new generation—a generation
born in America, educated at Harvard, and lacking deep
personal acquaintance with the Old World—was not to
build a city on a hill, but rather to perpetuate, nourish,
and defend a successful experiment in Puritan statecraft.
Samuel Willard shared with Increase Mather, the teacher
of the North Church, the intellectual leadership of this
new generation in Massachusetts.[16]

15. Ebenezer Pemberton, *A Funeral Sermon*, p. 70.
16. See Kenneth Ballard Murdock, *Increase Mather, the Foremost
American Puritan* (Cambridge, Mass., 1925); Robert Middlekauff, *The
Mathers: Three Generations of Puritan Intellectuals, 1596–1728* (New
York, 1971).

Shortly after moving to Boston, Willard began assisting the Reverend Thomas Thacher at the Third, or South Church, and in 1678 he was officially installed as the teacher, a position that he held until his death. Because his first wife had died, he soon married Eunice Tyng, who bore him fourteen more children. Through her he was connected with one of Boston's more prominent families; Eunice's father was a magistrate, and her sister was married to Joseph Dudley, who later became the governor of Massachusetts.[17]

Through his position and family Willard maintained close contact with many of the leaders in colonial society, especially with Judge Samuel Sewall. Willard, in fact, was the one who read publicly Sewall's confession of guilt for his participation in the infamous Salem witchcraft trial, an affair that Willard played a conspicuous part in terminating.[18]

Willard's emergence as the acting president of Harvard in 1701 grew out of a conflict between Increase Mather and the General Court. At the end of the century, when Increase Mather was president and Samuel Willard vice-president, the General Court decided that the presidency of the college was a full-time position. Mather in effect was forced to choose between being president of Harvard or teacher of North Church. After spending a miserable summer in Cambridge, Mather decided to resign and return to Boston. As vice-president Willard assumed the powers of the ranking officer of the college, yet was permitted to commute between South Church and Cambridge, precisely the type of arrangement denied to Increase Mather.[19]

17. Seymour Van Dyken, *Samuel Willard,* pp. 36–37.
18. Ola Elizabeth Winslow, *Samuel Sewall of Boston* (New York, 1964), pp. 133–36; Chadwick Hansen, *Witchcraft at Salem* (New York, 1969), pp. 240–41.
19. Samuel Eliot Morison, *Harvard,* pp. 530–40.

As one of the Bay Colony's major theologians, Willard was a prominent participant in the Reforming Synod of 1679/80, which approved "the adoption of the Savoy Confession, in practically unchanged form, as the creed of the Massachusetts churches." [20] The Savoy Confession of 1658 was in turn a revision by the Congregational Churches of England of the earlier and better known Westminster Confession.[21] Willard's lifework as the "Teacher of a Church in Boston" was structured by these normative statements of the Puritan faith.

While the burden of this study falls on *A Compleat Body of Divinity,* Willard's other theological works are important, and each deserves a few general comments, for some of them treat particular points even more extensively than does his magnum opus.

Willard's first major work, *Covenant Keeping* (1682), is derived from "several sermons, preached in order to solemn renewing of covenant." The preface by Increase Mather refers magisterially to the spread of opinion within the Reformed tradition at large on the question of "conditions" within the covenant of grace. For understanding the key categories at the heart of the Puritan synthesis, this is Willard's most helpful book.

Two years later Willard published two more big books, *Mercy Magnified* and *Child's Portion* (1684). The first covers the entire process of conviction and conversion, through a meticulous exegesis of the parable of the prodigal son, and the second focuses on "the unseen glory of the children of God" after the critical transition to the life of faith, hope, and love has been accomplished.

Heavenly Merchandize (1686) is Willard's fullest statement on the meaning of "Truth," and his *Brief Discourse*

20. Williston Walker, *The Creeds and Platforms of Congregationalism* (Boston, Mass., 1960), p. 421.

21. Ibid., pp. 340–402.

of Justification (1686) is his longest, sustained consideration of the meaning of justification by faith alone.

The *Doctrine of the Covenant of Redemption* (1694) carries the material implications of Willard's system to their logical conclusions as his speculative mind probes the inner workings of the Holy Trinity. The practical bearings of this abstruse account of how God the Father covenanted with God the Son for the redemption of the elect before the foundations of the world were laid are presented in *The Fountain Opened* (1700). The eternal love of God secured by the intertrinitarian covenant of redemption is made available to needful men through the covenant of grace.

The decisive distinction between being "externally" and "internally" related to the covenant of grace receives extended treatment in *Barren Figtree's Doom* (1691). *The Truly Blessed Man: or, The Way to be Happy Here, and For Ever* (1700) concerns those who are "internally" related to the covenant, and this is the largest single book Willard himself ever prepared for publication. Coupled with *Spiritual Desertions* (1699) and *The Christian's Exercise* (1701), *The Truly Blessed Man* expresses the profound tension within the consciousness of a justified sinner who has received the gift of grace and who remains perpetually on his way towards completion. *Sacramental Meditations* (posthumously published in 1711) is a celebration of the visible, sacramental signs God provides to sustain the Christian man throughout his pilgrimage.

In addition to these major works, Willard published at least eleven smaller treatises given "on the Lecture in Boston." Lecture day was a standard occasion for treating the meatier parts of the Puritan creed. The intelligentsia of the greater Boston area would normally be present to hear broader subjects addressed on a loftier level of abstraction than was typical on Sunday in the local congregations. The lecture day publications most central to Willard's thought are *Evangelical Perfection* (1694), *Law Established by the Gospel* (1694), and *Morality not to be Relied on for Life* (1700).

Nothing rivals in size or scope the marathon lecture series Willard began in 1688 and continued till his death in 1707. Once a month, on Tuesday afternoon, he meticulously worked his way through the Westminster Shorter Catechism. And like the medieval monks who never could finish writing the history of the world because they always started with the Creation, Willard died with the end only in sight. In the "Preface" to *A Compleat Body of Divinity* (posthumously published in 1726), the editors record the facts.

> Let the reader then be pleased to know, that the reverend author having gone through the explication of the assembly's Shorter Catechism in a more compendious manner among the children of his people, and having therein little more than methodized the subject and laid out the several heads to be more largely treated of; he did accordingly on Jan. 31. 1687,8 enter on these more elaborate discourses upon them. This he performed monthly on the Tuesday in the afternoon, in his public congregation; and so continued till April 1. 1707. soon after which he was prevented from proceeding by a fit of sickness, out of which he was scarce well recovered before he suddenly died.

> We must also here observe, that though the 220th lecture was the last the author delivered in public; yet in the midst of many avocations both from his numerous flock and the college, the weighty care of both together lying on him for several years before his death, he had most diligently redeemed his time and prepared about 26 others, even to the end of the 100th question, which contains the explication of the preface of the Lord's Prayer; when at the entrance of the petitions he was taken up to turn them to praises. Upon which account we have been obliged to supply the rest with his shorter exercises in his former expositions; where we therefore have a specimen of them, and may plainly see that

even they themselves, though so brief and so long since
made, yet were worthy of the light, if these larger ones had
not more agreeably superceded them. We should have been
glad indeed if the reverend author, who improved every
thing he took in hand, had finished the larger lectures on the
Lord's Prayer, and so gone through the seven remaining questions, and perfected the whole in a similar manner. But as
he himself observed when under apprehensions of being prevented from proceeding farther, there is the less need of
an exposition of this part of the catechism, since there's
scarce any subject of divinity that has been more frequently
considered by learned men; and we should therefore rather
adore the kindness of providence in bringing of our author
to so happy a period, than disesteem it as a defective labor.

Although Willard disappointed posterity by not finishing
in style, Thomas Prince and Joseph Sewall still judged this
series of lectures to be "one of the noblest and choicest
bodies of theoretical and practical divinity we have any
where met with, or we are apt to think has yet appeared
to the world." As the fullest statement of the Puritan synthesis in American colonial history, these editors gave
Willard's gigantic tome an appropriate title: *A Compleat
Body of Divinity in Two Hundred and Fifty Expository
Lectures on the Assembly's Shorter Catechism: Wherein the
doctrines of the Christian religion are unfolded, their
truth confirmed, their excellence displayed, their usefulness improved, contrary errors and vices refuted and exposed, objections answered, controversies settled, cases of
conscience resolved, and a great light thereby reflected on
the present age.*

CHAPTER TWO

Willard's "Systematical Divinity"

The articles of religion are delivered intelligibly, accommodable to the sentiments of human reason, and may be so understood, as the rules of other arts, by him that applies his mind to read, and hear, and study upon them. And there are no truths that have more rational confirmations given to gain men's credit, than than those of the Word of God. And though it be a great favor of God to make men orthodox in the points of divinity, and not leave them to a spirit of error; yet it is given to such as never come to a spiritual discerning. Christ supposeth that men may know their Lord's will, and not do it, Luke 12.47. And it is beyond question, that there are some who have a very large portion of knowledge in religion, who are yet utter strangers to the saving knowledge of Christ; whenas there are others whose knowledge of these things is more confused, who yet do so know God and Christ, as is eternal life.[1]

Theological education

Sometime during his tenure as the acting president of Harvard College, Samuel Willard circulated a small manuscript (posthumously published in 1735 by Thomas Prince

1. CB, p. 450.

and Joseph Sewall under the title, *Brief Directions to a Young Scholar Designing the Ministry, for the Study of Divinity*) in which he succinctly lays out the scope of theological education. Although the imperative mood predominates, it undoubtedly discloses Willard's own academic preparation for his lifework in theology.

After directing the young scholar to "be much in prayer to God for his help" and "put off high opinions of himself," Willard turns first to the Bible, which ought to be analyzed (1) grammatically in the original languages, (2) logically through "finding out the method of it, and the arguments contained in it," and (3) theologically by bringing diverse texts into "the analogy of faith." From scriptural interpretation Willard moves to "Systematical, or Common Place Divinity" that in turn leads to ethics where the various doctrines are applied to particular cases of conscience, and finally to "Polemical Divinity" in which all errors are refuted, for *"Quibus Argumentis Veritas astruiture, iisdem Falsitas Destruitur."* Furthermore, in his reading of "authors, whom God hath raised up . . . to be helpful to those that come after them" the young scholar should remember,

> The judgment of an able divine, may put him upon inquiry, but must not set him down: he must see the ground of all, and not *jurare in verba magistri:* else he will not be fit to convince others; for such authorities are no demonstrations.

Besides laying out the scope of the theological enterprise, Willard also offers some concrete directions on how to mark up "his own books" (but not the library's) and how to keep a "common-place book." [2] Willard's own huge 537-folio-page Commonplace Book is extant and provides a veritable index to the theological literature of the period.

2. BDYS, pp. 1–6.

When he began it cannot be precisely determined, for the first four pages have been destroyed, but it was probably set up before he left Harvard in 1662 and added to throughout his entire career. On the top of each page a different subject is written, with entries of author, book, and page listed below alongside more general notes. Sometimes passages are quoted and errors specified. The topical headings subdividing the doctrine of God are included to exhibit the comprehensive nature of Willard's Commonplace Book. (The numbers correspond to the page numbers in the manuscript.) [3]

9. Deus	30. Bonignitas
10. Dei Cognitio	31. Misericordia
11. Dei Sufficientia	32. Justitia Dei
12. Dei Essentia	33. Justitia Dei Remunerativa
13. Dei Existentia	34. Justitia Vindictiva
14. Dei Nomina	35. Redemptor
15. Dei Attributa	36. Attributa Positiva
16. Attributa Negativa	37. Sanctitas
17. Unitas	38. Vita Dei
18. Simplicitas	39. Intellectus Dei
19. Immensitas	40. Voluntas Dei
20. Infinitas	41. Libertas Dei
21. Incomprehensibilitas	42. Potentia Dei Absoluta
22. Aeternitas	43. Possibilitas and
23. Immutabilitas	Impossibilitas
24. Attributa Relativa	44. Potentia Ordinata Dei
25. Creator	45. Sapientia Dei
26. Conservator	46. Bonitas Dei and Gratia
27. Gubernator	47. Veritas and Fidelitas Dei
28. Dominium Dei	48. Gloria Dei
29. Omnipraesentia	49. Beatitudo Dei

3. Willard's "Commonplace Book" is in the Houghton Library at Harvard University.

Over and above keeping this larger Commonplace Book, Willard encourages the young scholar to "sometimes exercise himself in some particular common-place in divinity."[4] Here the student is directed

1. To pitch upon some text of scripture, which most clearly contains it [that is, the particular point of theology under question].
2. To clear up that scripture, and the sense of it, and accordingly to ground this theorem upon it.
3. To open the terms in it, and elucidate the meaning of the axiom, and give what needful distinctions may serve to determine the clear meaning of it.
4. To confirm it by scripture-arguments and testimonies.
5. To answer the objections, and refute the errors that have militated against it.
6. To draw the genuine inferences from it, whereby he may be confirmed in other truths which are confirmed by it.

Finally, the young scholar should "take opportunities to confer with others, especially orthodox and able ministers, about those points that are dark and difficult."[5]

Willard approaches theology as an art which is teleologically ordered exactly like every other art in the intellectual arena.

The end, though it be last in execution, yet is the first in intention; because, the better that is known, the fitter we are to judge of the other [i.e., the means]. A man cannot rationally tell what he is to do, until he first understand what it is for. Hence therefore all arts and sciences are wont to be defined by their ends: unto which, all that is delivered under them, is to be reduced; and the dignity, worth or excellency of every art, is thereby to be judged of.[6]

4. There is a second, 49-page "Commonplace Book" by Willard in the Houghton Library at Harvard University.
5. BDYS, pp. 6–7.
6. CB, p. 2.

As an academic discipline, theology's task is to order its subject matter around its stated end. Just to accept a number of theological beliefs will not do, for unless they are organized into a system through a "thinking in order," the mind will be trapped in "irrational and wild confusion, a perfect anarchy of thought, a mere harangue in language, unworthy [of] the excellent powers of men, and not agreeable to the nature and respect of things." [7]

What differentiates theology from other arts in the curriculum is the end it serves, and because that end is the most "excellent and desirable" end conceivable, Willard concludes (like the medieval schoolmen before him) that theology is the most sublime art. Theology was Queen in seventeenth-century Boston as well as in thirteenth-century Paris.

The most conspicuous "handmaiden" in the Queen's service is philosophy, or natural theology. (In seventeenth-century New England, the philosophical disciplines of metaphysics and ethics were frequently referred to by the medieval phrase "natural theology"; "natural philosophy," on the other hand, referred to scientific pursuits.) The relationship that holds between Willard's natural theology and his theology of revelation directly parallels his understanding of human happiness and Christian salvation.

The basic structural lines of Willard's system

On the initial page of *A Compleat Body of Divinity* Willard asserts that "the great thing which all rational, and immortal creatures have to be mostly inquisitive about, is HAPPINESS." The entire theological edifice Willard constructs is anchored in the natural yearnings of the human spirit for an infinite good that will satisfy "all the

7. CB, "Preface," p. iv.

reachings of the soul" and gratify "all its appetites." By nature man is so "insatiably desirous of happiness" that absolutely nothing can sever his deeper passions from this "congenerate principle of human nature." [8] Where animals unselfconsciously pursue their ends by instinct, man moves rationally and voluntarily, because he is "a reasonable creature" who "differs from, and excels the rest [of the visible world], and doth more nearly resemble the life of God." Man is a free, moral agent who must bid for his fulfillment.

> . . . freedom of will properly consists in a spontaneity, or liberty of choosing or refusing. It is the privilege of a cause by counsel, and it supposeth an understanding to direct, and a will to elect or reject accordingly. Such a freedom God did at first put into the angels and man; although it must always be considered in the subordination of a creature in the concourse or co-operation of God. And this freedom is the foundation of all moral transaction with such creatures.

Man sets a project before himself and freely follows his chosen path.

> Man can both propound to himself his own end, and make choice of the means or way leading unto it. He can deliberate with himself about these things, and take that which likes himself, and leave that which is not grateful unto him. None [and this includes God] can either compel or hinder him in his choice, but he can follow the dictates of his own understanding. From whence it follows, that all his human actions are voluntary and deliberate.[9]

Without exercising the power of reason and enjoying freedom of will, there could simply be no pursuit of happiness.

In order to achieve significant expressive power in a

---

8. SD, p. 69; CB, pp. 1, 30, 47, 182, 534, 716, 744; MM, p. 250.
9. CB, p. 185.

world of human meaning, moreover, one needs others, for man is "a dependent creature."

> Man is made a sociable creature, and the comfort of mankind is maintained by mutual intercourse and communion. . . . one man hath a great deal of dependence upon another, without which the affairs of this life cannot be carried on for the support of our livelihood; there are many things man wants, and there are many vocations that are needful for the supply of them; one man cannot carry on all by himself; and hence it comes to pass, that there is mutual traffic between men and transactions among them in the management of it. Nor can all things be carried so, as that there should be no more but present commutation, but men must trust one another; and therefore covenants and promises must pass between them for the future doing this or that, which may answer the ends of each. And that which makes these promises to pass for current between man and man, is truth in the promiser. It is the opinion of that which gives him credit with the other party; but for which opinion he would refuse to take his word or credit him on the value of it. If therefore there be a failure upon this account, mankind is disappointed; and if it should grow to be a common thing, the ligament of human society is dissolved and communities must be disbanded. If truth fail, all is put to a rout. If once a man cannot be believed, what should any others have any more to do with him? . . . It is indeed the ligature of all societies and if it be broken they will fall in pieces.[10]

Human existence in any meaningful sense is something one shares with others, not something one possesses on one's own, and this sharing requires promises among men to cover their future together. Stretching beyond the relative dependencies within the social world, furthermore, is man's "absolute dependence upon God." While one's so-

10. PK, p. 19.

ciety is the immediate context of one's life, society does not create the agent. That is God's work. Therefore, God is the inescapable Other upon whom every person is dependent absolutely and to whom each must answer for the life he holds in personal trust. To be human means that one stands in some personal, covenantal life-relationship to the absolute continuant within the divine-human community. The rapport with God spells the difference between ultimate joy and despair, final completion and alienation.[11]

According to Willard's reading of the story of the divine-human community, it is a story that begins in friendship, suffers a massive "falling out," and witnesses an overcoming of the rupture between the historical antagonists, God and man. The movement of thought in the body of Willard's "Systematical Divinity" commences with God, proceeds downwards—if spatial metaphors may be allowed—to the world and focuses upon man first as "a reasonable creature," then second as "a rebel," and third as the recipient of God's healing act of grace in Jesus Christ, who carries man to a final vision of God. In brief compass the previous sentence outlines the chapters that follow.

What needs to be specified here are three moments within the progression. First, the created world is correlative to God the Creator, and this forms the ontological structure of Willard's system. Second, man as "a reasonable creature" is correlative to God the Providential Governor, and this shapes the ethical moment in Willard's system. Together the ontology and ethics compose Willard's natural theology. But man is also "a rebel" who stands in need of reconciliation, and this introduces the religious stage, a stage which

11. See especially CE, entire; HG, p. 1ff; NS, p. 135; DJ, p. 16; BFD, p. 72; MC, p. 17; EP, pp. 179–81; MW, pp. 23–30; TBM, pp. 108, 293; FO, p. 99; SM, pp. 79–86; CK, p. 1; CB, p. 286.

turns upon a dialectic involving two vastly different "covenants" between God and man.

> It is an observation worth our serious minding, that ever
> since God made man upon the earth, he hath dealt with
> him in the way of a covenant. He was no sooner brought
> into the world, but was transacted with in this way. And
> when he had utterly lost himself by his disobedience to the
> first [covenant of works], then was a new and gospel covenant
> opened and revealed unto him, in that first glorious promise
> made after man's apostasy.[12]

If the covenant of works defines one's life-relationship
to God, then one is in either of these two religious states:
(1) *integrity* (Adam before the Fall), or (2) *apostasy* (all
fallen men lacking the favor of God). Needless to say, once
communion has been broken, it is impossible for man to
regain fellowship with God through the constitutional
order of the covenant of works. In order for fallen man to
become a completed being and enjoy communion with God,
Willard believes that it is necessary for him to become a
citizen within the new constitutional order God freely establishes through the covenant of grace. If this second
covenant defines one's life-relationship to God, then one
is in either of these two religious states: (3) *grace* (recipi-
ents of God's favor during this life), or (4) *glory* (the
saints in heaven).

At any given moment an individual human being exists in
the presence of God, *coram Deo,* within one of these four
religious states. Negatively put, there never has been or
ever will be a time when a person could possibly live outside of some one of these states. Although a man's religious
state may change, he can actually live in only one state
at a time. In principle this four-fold division is a comprehensive net designed to encompass the full range of re-

12. CK, pp. 1–2.

ligious possibilities open to human existence, and it is meant to demarcate radically different kinds of human situations in the presence of God.

When Willard moves from consideration of the essential nature of man as a reasonable creature to the concrete history of man's religious life-relationship to God, he enters a whole new realm of discourse which is significantly different in orientation and intention from his ontology and ethics. By introducing the covenant motif he effects a transition into confessional modes of thought in which the biblical witness exercises hegemony. Such a transition does not subtract anything from the natural theology: "that religion should contradict any maxim of the law of nature is unintelligible"; that which is "essential to his humanity" because it stems "from the principles of nature" is inseparable from human nature as such.[13] Rather it moves beyond the natural theology, not in the sense of leaving it behind, but in the sense of carrying it up into a personal perspective. It makes man's career through time interesting, a story to be told, a story of momentous encounters.

In summary, the structural lines of Willard's system run (1) from man's pursuit of happiness to God Transcendent, and (2) from fallen man's need for restoration within the divine-human community to God the Blessed Trinity: ". . . though one God be sufficient for the happiness of a creature, yet there must be three persons for the salvation of a sinner." [14] Willard's natural theology revolves on the former axis, and this side of the system is discernible from "the light of nature." Willard's confessional theology, on the other hand, revolves on the latter axis, and this side of the system is derived from the revelation contained in the plain Word of God.

---

13. MW, p. 13; CB, p. 125; cf. MRL, p. 8.
14. SM, p. 120; cf. CB, p. 100.

The light of nature

According to Willard's epistemology, knowledge is a relationship that joins together the knowing mind and the external world, and "the light of nature" involves a polarity
between the world and the mind that gains a cognitive
grasp of it. The degree of luminosity in nature's light, in
fact, is directly proportionate to the degree of union between subject and object: the greater the union, the more
radiant the light.

Basic to Willard's theory of knowledge is the conviction
that "man's nature inclines him to love knowledge in general." The mind is at home with reality: the "proper and
suitable object of the understanding is truth . . . in the
things that be."

> Truth . . . is firstly in him [God], and in them [creatures]
> only derivatively. The eternal idea which God had in his
> own infinite understanding, of all things that were to be in
> time, and all the several managements of them, is the ex-
> emplary truth. That which they have in themselves, is but a
> copy of this. Truth in the creature being its conformity unto
> that idea which God had of it in himself.[15]

The light of nature is grounded in God, visible through
the rational pattern of the given order of the universe,
and graspable by man's finite intelligence. Between the human mind and ultimate truth there stands an essential
point of contact in the natural world, a world which is
God's workmanship and man's theater of activity.

What man can know by this natural light is quite impressive. First, all the eternal laws of thought. Second, the
entire range of metaphysical wisdom that pagan philosophers in ancient Greece discovered independently of the

15. HM, p. 8; cf. CB, pp. 41, 91, 101–03, 108, 119, 120, 772; CR, p. 2;
CP, pp. 76–78, 89.

biblical revelation. Third, the moral law of the cosmos and man's obligation to obey it. And fourth, that man is "miserable, cursed, under a sentence of condemnation" for violating this moral order.[16] Regardless of how profoundly a soul or mind is disrupted, nature's light will not dim all the way out. Nevertheless, by following this light alone man never was, never is, and never will be capable of achieving communion with God, for that transcends nature's grasp. To be precise, even before Adam's fall, when there was not a trace of alienation between man and God, Adam in integrity still needed grace to effect the transition from the natural to the supernatural realm. And when estrangement came to characterize the human situation, a new creative act from the Creator was required to restore fellowship:

> How God should punish sin, and yet love the sinner; take vengeance on men's inventions, and yet extend grace to their persons, was above the discoveries of nature, a riddle beyond all its rule and principles to expound. It [nature] had its notions about *happiness*, but none about *salvation*.[17]

God's redemptive Word alone is a light sufficient to guide man into communion with God and felicity. And because this Word is found only in the Bible, the Holy Scriptures are the only suitable "rule of operation" to direct finite and fallen men towards their chief end.[18]

The plain Word of God

Willard's acknowledgment of the Old and New Testaments as the Word of God is very deliberately phrased. Within the Bible itself he finds four related but distinguish-

16. CB, p. 15; cf. pp. 445, 577–78; MM, p. 102.
17. CB, p. 16.
18. CB, p. 34; FO, p. 23; HM, p. 108; cf. WG, p. 35; CB, pp. 437, 452; SM, p. 120; MM, p 80; MRL, p. 11.

able denotations of "the Word of God": (1) the Eternal
Word or Son of God, the second person of the Trinity;
(2) God's eternal decrees through which he creates and
sustains the world; (3) God's providential governance of
the world; and (4) any disclosure of God's mind and will
to his people through a special revelation. And even this
fourth meaning, which is the one under consideration here,
is flexible, depending upon the stage of development among
the people of God. God saw fit to make himself known
efficaciously, in Willard's considered opinion,

> . . . sometimes by oracles, giving vocal commands to them;
> sometimes by Urim and Thummim; partly by angels appear-
> ing in human shape, and by the Son of God before his in-
> carnation, who often came to his servants of old; partly by
> visions and dreams, appearing to them in sleep, in raptures,
> and trances; and partly by prophets and extraordinary men
> sent and spirited by him; and partly by appointing such men
> to write down his will for the use of his people.[19]

In the infancy of the community of the covenant of grace
after the expulsion from the Garden of Eden, God taught
his children through oracles and angels, and during this
stage "revelation and tradition" shared equal status. Then
from the time of Moses until the coming of the Incarnate
Lord, "God instructed his church, partly by writings, and
partly by the continuance of revelation and tradition." The
circle narrowed after the time of Christ when the canon
of Holy Scripture was once and for all established: "the
whole mind of God (so far as concerns our direction to our
end) is there revealed; and now God treats men only by his
written Word." Why? Because the written Word alone is
a reliable disclosure of Jesus Christ. All the various passages

19. CB, pp. 13–15. According to the *Oxford English Dictionary*,
Urim and Thummim are "certain objects, the nature of which is not
known, worn in or upon the breast-plate of the Jewish high-priest by
means of which the will of Jehovah was held to be declared."

in the biblical witness "agree in Christ and center in him."
And since this one who is the veritable Word of God is
"contained in the Scriptures of the Old and New Testaments," the Bible, by way of a "metonymical expression,"
can legitimately be called the Word of God.[20] When Willard states that the Bible is "the rule of operation" for the
art of theology, his controlling idea is that Jesus Christ the
Word of God is the "way to eternal life" and that he is
attested to throughout the entire Bible. The Book is ap-
proached with ultimate seriousness simply because God's
Word of salvation is "therein *contained* and no where
else." The Bible's authority, quite obviously, is derivative
and not self-authenticating. It is not God—it cradles the
authentic Word from the Father. As Increase Mather put
it in his Preface to Willard's *A Brief Discourse Concerning that Ceremony of Laying the Hand on the Bible in
Swearing,* "But though we ought to reverence the blessed
Bible above all other books, yet we may not worship it,
but the author of it only." [21]

While this is sufficient to indicate the christological and
soteriological determination of Willard's doctrine of the
written Word, the hermeneutical principles underlying his
interpretation of the Bible will exhibit the disciplined
character of his reading. To acknowledge that "saving
knowledge" is deposited in the Bible is to go only halfway.
"Truth is not to be laid up in chests, and coffers . . . but
it is the understanding of man, which is the only subject
of truth; we have it, when we know it." A biblical passage
must be understood in order to be effectual, and to unlock
the written Word so that it will be "directing" instead of
"perplexing" requires skill as well as prayer.[22]

The pivotal principle of Willard's hermeneutics is

20. CB, pp. 13, 14, 20; cf. pp. 579, 614.
21. LHB, "Preface"; CB, p. 23.
22. HM, p. 18; CB, p. 30.

God's "accommodating of himself to our capacity." [23] Because God has "condescended to write heavenly truths in
earthly language," using "for the most part plain men, such
as were not adorned with human literature," a diversity of
styles and intentions is manifested throughout the Bible.
Some passages are designed "to inform the understanding,"
others "to engage the will," and still others "to move upon
the affections." Shining through all this diversity, however, the "plain" truth is sufficiently "perspicuous" to "direct men in their work, to show what is to be done, and
how to do it." Willard does proceed to point out that
"many things spoken in Scripture . . . are altogether above
the comprehension of a created understanding" because they
are "too big for us to imbibe," but as "a rule of operation"
for the art of theology what the Bible discloses is "easy and
intelligible." [24]

Because the plain Word must be grasped through the
Bible's manifest diversity, Willard breaks down a given
passage through analysis to arrive at the heart of the
matter, and then through synthesis gathers the results into
a unified system of beliefs.

The analysis operates with the four-fold levels of meaning common to the medieval mind, and the sense Willard
is intent upon pursuing for his theological task is the "literal
sense." When he plays the "literal sense" against "the alle-
gorical, tropological and anagogical senses" he is insisting
on the proper, objective meaning of a text; indeed, he
sometimes even refers to it as the "historical sense," though
"literal" predominates. For the purposes of academic and
exact scholarship only that sense which the writer of a
given passage meant is significant. To fall back upon the
other levels of interpretation would be to surrender the

23. HM, p. 2; BFD, p. 3; BDYS, p. 2; SM, pp. 5, 121.
24. CB, pp. 30–31; cf. HM, p. 101.

scientific, historical character of exegesis. Furthermore, even the literal sense is not to be accepted "literalistically" in any simple-minded way. The Old South congregation was informed directly that

> . . . though the things concerning God, which are revealed in the Scriptures, are not false, but true, yet they are infinitely short of expressing his sublimity, and they are very improper. We must always remember that God is inconceivably more, and better, than all that is or can be said of him. And it may also teach us to have a care how far we strain the human expressions of Scripture, in drawing of conclusions from them, concerning the nature of God.[25]

And the literal, historical meaning, moreover, does not exclude the other senses categorically, but it should keep them under proper control in their appropriate homiletical and devotional situations.[26]

Even after a given text is analysed, however, obscurity may still cloud the beautiful face of truth, but if such an apparently unclear passage is interpreted in the light of "those which are more plain," then all difficulties should subside. The golden rule for synthesizing the results of logical exegesis is that "Scripture is its own best interpreter." And the theological intention of exegesis is to build up "foundation principles" from the biblical witness into "an analogy of faith." [27]

> The whole body of divine truths is uniform. Truth is but one, whereas error is manifold. Truth is self-consenting, but error is self-contradicting. There is a sweet harmony in the whole Word of God. There are no contradictions to be found there. If any shall judge that there are such, the mistake is

25. CB, p. 45.
26. Cf. CB, p. 32; SD, p. 12; FO, p. 44; BDYS, p. 3; BFD, p. 146; HM, p. 2.
27. BDYS, p. 3; CB, p. 33; cf. MM, p. 381.

not in the Scriptures, but in their deceived understandings.
. . . So that whensoever you meet with two doctrines, between which you observe a manifest inconsistency, you may
and must conclude, that both of these cannot possibly be
true, and also that that must be so, which is consonant with
the whole analogy of faith, or the body of saving truths.[28]

This integrative procedure undoubtedly deprived Willard's
biblical studies of the richness that comes from a more
literary approach to the text. Although Willard's four un-
published and apparently lost commentaries on the Psalms,
Romans, Corinthians, and Galatians might alter this judgment somewhat, his published expositions of biblical passages, such as *Mercy Magnified,* indicate that theological
interests take priority in his actual exegetical method.

Such an integrative method, it should be mentioned,
does not reduce all the teachings derived from the Bible
to a homogeneous mass of equally important assertions.
While all biblical truths may be "suitably and profitably
applied" because they are all "precious and God's ministers are not to shun declaring the whole counsel of God,"
Willard balances this with two basically different considerations. The first is pragmatic: "there are some times when
some truths are not to be delivered, because unseasonable,
in that God's people are not prepared to receive them." [29]
The second consideration is more fundamental in that
Willard believes that some truths are more important because they stand nearer than others to the core of the
Christian message: "there are some that are so essential to
piety, that the denial of them undermines the very foundation of Christianity." [30] In this context the "various ends
and uses" manifested in the Bible, which "consists of divers
parts," take on further significance.

28. HM, pp. 113–114.
29. TBM, p. 430; CE, p. 180.
30. PT, p. 27.

There are recorded in it [the Bible] many histories, and these serve partly for holy example, and partly for solemn caution to men. There are moral precepts, there are sharp reproofs, there are severe threatenings, etc., all of which have their particular profit, and will serve, either to the preparing of a sinner for this closure with Christ by faith, or for the helping of a believer home to the heavenly kingdom. But that which nextly and most properly gives us the advantage and encouragement to believe in Christ, is that special revelation which God hath been pleased to make of him, in the which revelation he gives us to understand, that as he is a complete and all sufficient Savior, so he invites sinners to come to and accept of him, and put their trust in him, and engageth to all such as so do, that they shall in and by him obtain the pardon of sin, and peace with God; that if they will but take Christ on his terms, he shall be theirs.[31]

The Bible is composed of several types of writings, each with different intentions and varying degrees of religious value, and the greatest of these gravitate around the restoration of communion within the divine-human community.

The Spirit and Puritan experience

Given the light of nature, the plain Word of God, the learned tools of exegesis, and a well-regulated method, if the seeker's heart is filled with nothing more than these can provide, then "he hath but trifled." "All the literal light that men get by study, hath no heat in it; it doth not engage the heart at all in love to God." Until "the soul hath tasted that God is gracious, hath felt the bitterness of sin, and been distrest by reason of the wrath of God, and known the grace of God in giving him repentance and pardon," in brief, until a man "can set the seal of his experience to it," all the theological notions that he may hold in his

---

31. DJ, p. 83; cf. CB, p. 246.

head and profess with his lips, even though they may be true, are insufficient for a man's yearning for completion. Theology is similar in this regard to other intellectual disciplines: "a mere discursive knowledge of any art makes a man but a bungler, compared with one that hath been practiced in it." [32]

Lest Willard's elevation of "feeling" over "thought," or "practice" over "mere discursive knowledge" be interpreted as some kind of anti-intellectualism, it should be noted that Willard places the understanding, not the will, in the commanding position: "Now the natural motion of the will in man, is by the light of the understanding." Or in a fuller statement of this position, Willard declares:

> All human actions are deliberate, in which the understanding is employed, and the will is determined according to the verdict of it. There must therefore be some motive to invite and excite the man to consent, in order to his being prevailed upon.[33]

Interestingly enough, Willard's intellectualism even leads him to forsake the traditional Augustinian motif of "faith seeking understanding."

> Now the soul is not first made to believe, and then see the reason of it, but the Spirit of God draws the soul to believe, by making it see the excellency of the object, and so persuading it. He is first made to see the ground of hope, and then to follow.[34]

Willard holds the emotions and the mind together by subordinating the heart to the head. From this it does not follow and is not true that the heart is unimportant. But it does follow that in any given sermon the "doctrinal"

32. HM, p. 18; TBM, pp. 416–17, 422; PT, p. 20; SM, p. 21.
33. DJ, p. 86; CE, p. 17; cf. HM, p. 19; DP, p. 5; TBM, p. 470; MM, p. 150.
34. MM, p. 191; cf. 149.

section comes before and prepares the way for the "applicatory."

> The first is doctrinal, consisting in laying open the truth, so as the understanding may apprehend it, and be made to give its assent to it. We must have a conception and a conviction of it, and this must go before application, being to prepare for it. And therefore to fall to application before the truth be explained, and proved, is to make confusion. The second is applicatory, which takes the truth so laid open and improves it for our benefits in the service of God.[35]

And in like manner "faith" forms the foundation for "obedience" or "duty" in the systematic formulation of "the whole circle of religion." [36]

After insisting upon the idea that "to raise the affections, without informing the mind, is a fruitless unprofitable labor, and serves to make zeal without knowledge," Willard proceeds to argue that theology, like true repentance, "rests not in thoughts and purposes, but proceeds to practice." Theology in fact is a highly practical art whose very "design . . . is to teach men to live to God." And in the active life the affections should be "let out upon" that which the intellect pronounces good. The means to the right end are to be pursued passionately, and Willard even grants that "the best way to raise" the affections of others "is to express our own." A man purchases the "heavenly merchandize" and takes "possession of the truth" only "when the soul, discerning of a transcendent beauty in it, and persuaded of the incomparable worth of it, prefers it before all other things whatsoever, and parting with everything else, in heart and affection, closeth in with it, and Christ in it, as the only soul satisfying portion." [37]

---

35. TBM, pp. 423–25.
36. CB, "Preface," p. i, pp. 2, 33–37, 559.
37. TBM, pp. 418, 423–25; MM, pp. 150, 273; HM, p. 18.

In saying all this, however, Willard does not mean that if and when the rational soul firmly grasps the goodness of an object that the whole man always loves it. Within the natural realm this is true, but in the supernatural the will does not automatically follow the judgment of the understanding. Over and beyond the requirement that man must know the good in order to do it, when this involves man's supernatural vocation, the Spirit must act. "Theoretical knowledge is not to be neglected, being the first step to true wisdom," but it is still the case that "it is not to be rested in, because it is not that knowledge which is eternal life." While necessary, it is hardly sufficient, for the Holy Spirit alone can effect such a closing in with God's truth that the "literal light" discovered by the discursive reason is transformed into "saving" and "practical" wisdom. The "illumination of the Spirit" does not compensate for any deficiencies in the written Word of God; it opens the blind eyes of man's reason to it and animates his will to love and serve the God who condescends to make himself known through it.[38]

In the presence of God, the Puritan who is properly and powerfully moved by the Holy Spirit experiences two fundamental feelings: (1) a profound sense of personal *guilt* for mankind's acts of treason against the sovereign lordship of God over his workmanship, and (2) an overwhelming sense of *gratitude* for God's forgiving and restoring grace. Correlative to these two sides of a believer's awareness are, respectively, the holiness and grace of God. Man is responsible for all disorder and evil in the universe; God is to be praised for all goodness and harmony. To bring his congregation to acknowledge these truths is the dominant thrust in much of Willard's preaching. And to maintain the proper balance between guilt and gratitude in the

38. CB, pp. 32, 58, 326–27, 426, 450ff; WG, p. 35; BFD, p. 133; FO, p. 130.

life of a justified sinner and show how God's holiness and grace are ultimately united in God is one of the most frequently addressed nests of problems in all of Willard's published works.

Faith and reason

From the light of nature Willard concludes that all creation owes its existence to the Divine Workman, that man's ultimate love ought to center in God or Goodness Itself, and that man stands condemned for violating the natural law written in his own heart and offending the holiness of the transcendent majesty of his Maker and Sustainer. The Bible, on the other hand, teaches that this same God compassionately condescends to man in his need, rectifies the natural order, and carries the creature into eternal felicity. The rebellious one, through God's gracious act, can enjoy communion with the Holy One. Where nature's light leads to guilt, the biblical witness points to gratitude. Where reason should acknowledge man's offensiveness, faith alone can receive God's acceptance of him who has gone whoring after false gods.

Because Willard's "Systematical Divinity" synthesizes materials drawn from two sources, one source knowable by right reason, the other received in faith, how he relates faith and reason needs to be specified. In order to understand the relationship it is necessary first to realize that one and the same God discloses his mind and heart to man in two fundamentally different ways, and that both ways are God's revelation of himself. Although "revelation" tends to be reserved for the biblical revelation, this is only a tendency. Technically, God reveals himself through both his works and Word. God's works arise from his creating and sustaining power and constitute "nature." The book of nature, which is open to all men, is God's general or natural revelation of himself. Over and beyond this stands God's special or salvific Word to his chosen people contained in the Bible. The Christian theologian treats both types of disclosures from the same God.

The second point is that every truth from God's special revelation is compatible with God's general revelation. "Compatible with" is used deliberately to exclude any contradictions between the two, and to include specifiable differences between them. According to Willard, God's special revelation goes beyond the general in the sense of providing further information, but nothing derived from the special can falsify the general. Exactly put, it is impossible for any two propositions that are grounded in God's being and known through either general or special revelation to be such that if one is true the other must be false.

In the third place, what faith receives through special revelation is also knowledge. Faith does not become noncognitive even when its subject matter transcends the grasp of right reason. As Willard puts it at one place, "though God be to be seen by an eye of faith, yet he must be seen by an eye of reason too; for though faith sees things above reason, yet it sees nothing but in a way of reason." [39]

In the light of these overarching points, it is possible to demarcate three different types of propositions within Willard's system. First, some propositions are discoverable through the light of nature, open to inspection by all men, and are philosophically justifiable. Taken as a whole they constitute Willard's natural theology. It is propositions of this sort that figured in the questions debated at Harvard commencements (and by implication taught in Harvard's philosophy courses). Willard's fullest theoretical treatment

39. CB, p. 50; cf. p. 44; MW, p. 13.

of this type of proposition, in fact, occurred, in a controversy occasioned by such an exercise. George Keith had attended the 1702 commencement at Harvard and was outraged when in the customary academic debate it was concluded that the immutability of God's eternal decrees and the liberty of man as a reasonable creature were not mutually exclusive, or in the language of the schools, their "compossibility" was affirmed. To Keith this was tantamount to claiming that God was the author of evil, and lest his silence be interpreted as tacit consent he wrote out his objections and sent them to Willard. Because they were written in Latin Willard at first ignored them (assuming that only educated persons could read them and consequently could also easily spot the fallacies), but when Keith started passing them around in plain English Willard's hand was forced. As the ranking officer of Harvard College he felt compelled to answer Keith's "manifest design, not only to render my person obnoxious, but to expose the academy itself to odium." [40]

One of the more interesting things in Willard's *Brief Reply to Mr. George Keith* is his observation on the ground rules of a commencement exercise, ground rules which Keith had violated by bringing in nonphilosophical arguments:

> This question was, *pro more*, to be debated philosophically, or according to the light of nature, and the principles of natural theology: in which the respondent was to defend the consistency of these two [propositions], by the strength of reason; whereas the opponent's province was to attempt the making it to appear that they are inconsistent; and that either there must be no decree, or that not immutable, or the reasonable creature must lose its freedom: for the defence

40. BRGK, p. 2.

of which principles, against the arguments, and instances brought to undermine them, it is necessary to use such reasons, and offer such distinctions, as may be supposed agreeable to right reason, and to the nature of the things disputed on: the profitableness of which sort of disputations on such occasions, is pleaded by the practice of all the academies in Christendom.[41]

Willard's understanding of the immutability of God's eternal decrees, and the nature of human freedom, and by implication the order of the world, is a piece of natural theology.

It should be pointed out, however, that these philosophical points might also be supported by biblical authority. For example, the temporality of the world is philosophically demonstrable from the light of nature, and yet the Bible also states this truth authoritatively. When a given proposition can be derived from both sources, Willard's characteristic procedure is to argue this point philosophically and then cap it with a proof-text to reinforce that which is naturally knowable. But sometimes he merely leaves it with a statement such as, "And for this, reason will suffice, and we need not go to revelation for it." [42]

At the opposite end of the spectrum stand the mysteries of the faith which are derived solely from God's special revelation and cannot be rationally accounted for.

Now a mystery is a thing that is abstruse and secret. We have a notion of the thing itself, but are at a loss about the way and manner of it. We cannot understand or express how it was brought about. The mystery of the trinity of persons in the unity of the God-head; of the two natures infinitely disproportionable in themselves, united in the person of Christ; and of the union of a believer to Christ in regeneration, are depths, which the line of our understanding is not able to

41. Ibid., p. 7.
42. CB, pp. 3, 653.

fathom; but after our utmost search, we must sit down to
gaze upon them with admiration.[43]

Even though a mystery transcends the grasp of man's finite
mind, even when it is illumined by the Holy Spirit, this
definitely does not mean that a mystery is irrational or that
the devout mind should not attempt to penetrate it
through "our utmost search." The believer in fact does
have "a notion of the thing itself," but while he can apprehend the mystery and rationally see that it does not
violate any canon of reason, still it is not, in the technical
meaning of the term, comprehensible. Exactly put, even
though a saint might rationally rise to a lofty point in his
understanding of a mystery, it is impossible for his finite
mind to understand fully a mystery's content or to give
a purely rational account of it. Obviously a mystery, then,
is simply an article of faith.

In between these two extremes, furthermore, stands a
third type of proposition that shares characteristics with
each, yet is not reducible to either. Some propositions are
disclosed only through God's special revelation and yet they
differ from mysteries in that once they are revealed the
finite mind can understand them—they do not introduce
conceptual difficulties for right reason. As Willard puts it
in one revealing sentence, "though the light of nature told
him [man] that the world he came into was God's workmanship; yet it did not of itself say how much time God
took up, in the creation of it; for God could have done all
things with one word, in an instant; and therefore the distinct knowledge of this is a matter of faith." [44] Whether God
created the world in a flash, in six days, or over millions of
years can be adjudicated only through biblical authority,
but given the actuality of the world and God's manifest

43. CB, p. 429; cf. pp. 31, 35; BRGK, p. 18.
44. CB, p. 660; cf. pp. 110–11.

creativity, every answer is equally credible. This third type
is composed of all those propositions that are derived from
the Bible but still remain in that realm of possibility that
can be rationally accounted for.

In summary, virtually everything Willard wrote is concerned with the doctrines of faith, but within his "Systematical Divinity" reason operates on three distinguishable
levels. First, reason can comprehend and explain all the
truths disclosed by God through the light of nature. Second, reason can cope with all those biblical truths that
remain in the realm of possibility that can be rationally
accounted for. And third, reason can apprehend mysteries
and see that they do not violate right reason, and yet reason
finally must "sit down to gaze upon them with admiration," for they are "depths which the line of our understanding is not able to fathom."

Although Willard's vital concern as a Christian minister
lies with the mysteries of the faith in which the merciful
Redeemer rescues fallen man from his self-imposed plight
("the ABC of Christianity"),[45] he approaches the history
of God's dealings with man and man's responses to God's
initiative within the framework of nature. The Redeemer-
believer relationship is encompassed by the Creator-creature
relationship which secures the possibility for, and sets the
limits to, the redemptive story.

45. HM, p. 108.

CHAPTER THREE

God the Master Workman

*It is of infinite concernment, that we be rightly fixed
on the object of worship; for if it be not such an one
as can make us happy, our religion is vain. That there
must be a God, the light of nature discovers, and
therefore all nations do acknowledge it.*[1]

The existence of God

Man's ultimate concern for an infinite good dialectically
negates anything other than God as being capable of happi-
fying man, because God alone is sufficient for the nature
of man. "No created thing can satisfy the reachings of man's
will." "Man, as he is a reasonable creature, stands in need
of a deity to make him happy." [2] But does God exist? Is
there any power that transcends the world of created being?

Theologians within the Reformed tradition at large seldom expend much time or energy demonstrating the existence of God as "the most Absolute First Being." Gilbertus
Voetius (1589–1676), for example, cautions that "before the
ruder and weaker and in catechetical instructions . . . it
will as a rule be sufficient to assume" the existence of God.
The Westminster Shorter Catechism even omits the ques-

1. CB, p. 94.
2. CB, pp. 46–49.

tion altogether. And the very first sentence of John Norton's
The Orthodox Evangelist (1657), surely one of the more
impressive treatises written by a New England theologian
during the first generation, simply asserts that "though
nothing is more manifestly known, than *that* God is; yet
nothing is more difficultly known than *what* God is,"
thereby moving directly into a discussion of the essence of
God and prescinding from the prior question of whether
or not God is. Voetius, however, does proceed to add that
in "academical instructions and disputations . . . theologians should be armed against antagonists of every kind.
But this should be done with such care and circumspection,
that it does not appear to be an airing of a dialectical
problem." [3] The suspicion of course is that discursive proofs
for God's existence engender doubt. But another reason
why the issue is seldom faced directly by Puritan intellectuals arises from their conviction that philosophical atheism was not a serious or widespread threat. "Whether there
be any thorough professed atheist in the world, who doth
absolutely deny the being of a God," Willard informs his
auditors, "is questioned by many, and may so be with a
great deal of reason; and if there have any such been, . . .
they have justly been accounted prodigies," who apparently
lacked even the dim intelligence of an ordinary reprobate.
("Practical atheism," however, which theoretically acknowledges the existence of God but then proceeds to deny it
through everyday conduct, is a different matter; "atheism"
almost always is used by Willard in this practical sense.)[4]
That God exists is so indisputable in Willard's mind that
he backs into a discussion of the issue with an apology:
"It may here perhaps seem a thing superfluous to go about

3. Heinrich Heppe, *Reformed Dogmatics* (London, 1950), pp. 47–48;
John Norton, loc. cit., emphasis added, and "then" altered to "than."
4. CB, pp. 603–04.

to prove a truth so clear and manifest as this, which is the prime dictate of nature's light." [5]

Besides exploiting the customary homilectical arguments based on the amazing survival of the church in the face of implacable adversity, the ignominious downfall of scoffers, and the interior testimony of a condemning conscience that contradicts the notion that man could be "the supreme regulator of his own actions," Willard philosophically approaches the problem of God's existence through the exterior route from the world to God, using a posteriori arguments. Even though the whole creation is an empty wasteland when pitted against the infinite reachings of the human heart for completion, it nevertheless points towards the God who can satisfy this need authentically.

The entire cosmological hierarchy, with its plethora of gradations, has quantity (place), duration (time), and contingency (it could not-be). With these essential characteristics it follows that the world cannot be accounted for in terms of itself alone. We know through simple observation that the world is "subject to change" and therefore is "a creature of time." Temporality dictates that there must be a beginning. But before the beginning "it was not," and therefore could not "give being to itself," for "efficiency presupposeth an existence, which the world had not, when it was not." Consequently, either there is "an omnipotent power, before and beyond the creature, that must be the author of this great work," or there would be no world. That there is, is obvious, so this "commands our acknowledgment of an increated power, and that is God." Through the cosmological route Willard concludes that the given world requires a creative ground of being that is necessary in and of itself.[6]

5. CB, p. 37.
6. CB, pp. 37–38, 59, 109.

Not only does the created order derive its being through participation in a transcendent ground; its very composition is so ingenious and harmonious that nothing less than an omniscient intelligence could so organize the cosmos. Even a lowly "worm, or a pile of grass" displays an intentional order. Fresh from the microscope Willard rhapsodically reports that "there are some insects so small, that our sight cannot discern them, without the help of a glass, and that yet they should have in them all the organs of sense and motion, is astonishing." But more to the point is "the harmony of the whole [universe] in all its parts." Could any mind think that anything less than an "infinite wisdom" would be capable of keeping "this great machine" in working order? That "there is nothing vain, or useless, or incapable of being serviceable in its place" in "this curious watch" of a world, testifies to a workman who must exercise extraordinary powers. Because even "unreasonable creatures are guided to attain such ends, that they know not of," Willard argues that they must be "guided by one above them, who knows both their journey's end, and the way to it." From the teleological drive exhibited in the universe as a whole and in its various parts, Willard concludes that there must be an ultimate, self-sufficient end which directs and fulfills all that exists.[7]

God, hidden and revealed

Even though all contingent reality participates in a transcendent ground and points towards a self-sufficient end, Willard carefully explains that this absolute is radically different from everything else and in principle is not simply the greatest one within a field of many. God "is not a being properly, as we conceive of a being; much less a portion of

7. CB, pp. 38, 66; cf. pp. 109, 118, 121, 130.

being, as a thing which may be defined is; but he is above being." Indeed, "the first being must of necessity be *being itself*." And because the chasm that separates being itself from any and all finite being is "an infinitely vast distance," God can never become an object of thought strictly so-called. He is "incomprehensible" and "ineffable." Consequently, between man's mind and God's essential being as he is in himself and known only to himself—"the naked essence of God"—a veil is drawn which never can be pierced, not even in the beatific vision of the state of glory.[8]

The reason why the mind can never penetrate the hidden essence of God lies in the epistemological principle that the mind cannot rise above its own level of knowing.

> The thing known is in the knower, according to the manner, and measure of him that knows, and therefore the knowledge of every one is accommodated to the manner of his own nature, and not according to the manner of the nature of the thing known.[9]

From this it logically follows that the finite mind can never span the infinite gap between the creature and the Creator to "entertain the *quidditative* conception" of the hidden essence of God which is known only to God himself. That Willard takes his epistemology seriously can be seen in his further argument that "God cannot reveal and make known to the creature his innate perfection," for such a creature capable of receiving the full "latitude and glory" of God's inner being would have to exercise the powers of a divine mind. And this would be tantamount to claiming that the uncreated one created another uncreated power, which obviously "would imply a contradiction." Furthermore, to know God directly would be "altogether destructive"; a mere glimpse of God's "most glorious and illustrious" face

8. CB, pp. 40, 42–43, 49–51, 56; CP, pp. 129ff.
9. CB, p. 41.

with its dazzling "oriental brightness" would obliterate man's creatureliness.[10]

Although God cannot (and mercifully will not) allow the finite mind to know the divine essence as God knows himself, God is not locked in a prison of his own internal being with its innate perfection. God can and in fact does reveal himself to man's finite capacities by refracting his inner being through the prism of the world. The analogy Willard uses to make this *indirect* approach more understandable is taken from the book of nature:

> Now if we fix our eyes directly on the body of the sun, it will wholly dazzle us; but if we look on the reflected light or beams of it, we are safe, and it is comfortable.[11]

What man perceives when he beholds God's revealed essence (or as Willard is wont to express it, God's "backparts") is only "a very little portion of him" scaled down to the measure of a finite intelligence.

> God's discoveries of himself to us are therefore some small part of his great excellencies, and when we have said all that we can to set him forth, how little will it be in comparison of himself! It will not bear the proportion that one drop doth to the sea. . . . It [a creaturely mind] may be swallowed up in the glory of God. It may swim in the ocean of everlasting bliss. It may be contained, but it can contain no more than its own measure. A vessel that is full, cannot be more full.[12]

Even that "more full and perfect knowledge that we shall have in heaven" will forever be "limited and circumscribed to the manner and measure of the created understanding." [13]

10. CB, pp. 41–42.
11. CB, p. 43.
12. CB, p. 44.
13. CB, pp. 42–45.

Since the distinction between the finite creature and the infinite Creator is ultimate, human knowledge in principle can only be indirect, and this in turn entails that all human discourse concerning God will always remain improper and inadequate. A finite mind can think only by joining a subject and predicate together "by a compound act." Therefore, the Absolute whose "nature is simple, and altogether void of any sort of composition" necessarily transcends the grasp of human expression. Furthermore, the superabundance of God's disclosed essence requires man to say numerous things in order to state the approximate truth about that which by definition is singular.

Given this cognitive situation a question is posed in this acute form: do the multifarious distinctions in the finite mind correspond in any way to transcendent reality? If yes, then how could God be purely simple? If no, then how could human language ever be reliable when speaking about God?

Willard cuts through this dilemma by stating first that the distinctions in the mind ("in reason *reasoning*") are objectively grounded in God's disclosure of himself ("in reason *reasoned*"). In accommodating himself to man's capacities God "takes the rational or logical arguments upon himself, admits of a distinction or a description, utters sentences or actions about himself, speaks of himself *as if* he were an effect and had causes; a subject, and had adjuncts." (Emphasis added.) The fullness of the divine essence, moreover, is refracted into numerous perfections which "shine forth after a distinct manner." The revealed essence of God "comes into our understanding, under a various representation, . . . as through so many glasses." This multiplicity, while objective to man's mind, however, is not of such a nature that it destroys God's inner unity. Strictly speaking, "there can be no division or proper distinction in his [God's] being." God is really *one* and yet his perfections are objectively distinct in his disclosure of himself, "as the sun by one and the same light, enlightens, warms, hardens, softens, nourishes and dries up things; as all lines meet in their center, in one individual point; as all waters are one in the sea." God is not one behind the manifold perfections: he is one squarely within them, for "whatsoever is in the divine essence, is most properly the divine essence." Therefore, "his mercy is God, and his justice is God; and they are both one and the same undivided God." From this it follows that there can never be any ultimate "clashing" among the multiple perfections that are formally distinct within the singular essence of God. Man's mouth is not shut, but he must speak many times in order to express the fullness of the one God. The "as if" limits all human discourse about God Transcendent.[14]

By employing this "as if" Willard opens a middle way between a *real* distinction (in which two things are physically separable) and a *mental* or *notional* or *virtual* distinction (in which the division is purely within the mind, e.g., the distinction between "man" and "rational animal").[15] And this allows him to stress the infinite qualitative difference between the Creator and creature without pushing it so far as to vitiate all rational knowledge and reduce man completely to some non-verbal awareness of the Wholly Other. For example, in attempting to gain a cognitive grasp of the most abstract of all abstractions, *being itself*, Willard finally reverts to that which is humanly manageable:

> Because being is better than not being, we ascribe being to God; *as if* he had something in common with other beings, or *as though* there were a general nature, in which

14. CB, pp. 41–42, 50, 51, 54, 62, 65, 72; cf. pp. 218, 450; CR, p. 69; TBM, pp. 266, 394.
15. Cf. F. C. Copleston, *A History of Philosophy,* 2: pp. 508ff.

there were an agreement or participation between him, and the creature; and it is a notion, without which we can entertain no conception of God at all. (Emphasis added.)[16]

It should be emphasized that the cognitive situation is the same regardless of the source of man's knowledge of God. The biblical revelation, while it discloses further truth, is just as bound by this limitation as the book of nature:

. . . though the things concerning God, which are revealed in the Scriptures, are not false, but true, yet they are infinitely short of expressing his sublimity, and they are very improper. We must always remember that God is inconceivably more, and better, than all that God is or can be said of him. And it may also teach us to have a care how far we strain the human expressions of Scripture, in drawing of conclusions from them, concerning the nature of God.[17]

Even though human language is not commensurable with the divine object and therefore cannot express the plenitude of the divine essence in propositions which hold a one-to-one relationship to ultimate reality, what man knows about God through the natural order and the Bible is not false and must be relied upon, for that is all that ever will be available. God is knowable only in his disclosure of himself through his works and Word.

The multiple perfections of the transcendent one

What man indirectly knows about his Maker in the first instance is that the transcendent one contains within his simple essence "the whole and universal fullness of all perfection to the utmost latitude of possibility." These multitudinous perfections, according to Willard's distribution,

16. CB, p. 49.
17. CB, p. 45.

fall into two basic patterns. On the one hand, there are those metaphysical perfections (such as eternality) which are appropriate only to God without even a shadow in the sphere of creaturely being. On the other hand, there are those moral perfections (such as goodness) which are appropriate to God supereminently and yet also are applicable to creatures in a lesser degree. Technically the former are "incommunicable," while the latter are "communicable."

The incommunicable perfections Willard explicitly treats are God's infinity (under which immensity and omnipresence are subsumed), eternality, and immutability. Each of these attributes, which are found only in the divine essence, is derived by stripping away those features of the given universe of experience which are unworthy of absolute perfection. The world is finite, temporal, and mutable —that is what it means to be a contingent creation. By negating these essential characteristics of all beings that are dependent upon another for their existence, the mind rises through a negative route to a knowledge of what God is not. In knowing that God is not such and so, the mind gains only negative awareness—a positive content for these incommunicable perfections cannot be formed in a finite mind.[18]

To exhibit Willard's use of this negative method it will suffice to consider only one perfection, eternality. Beginning with time, Willard defines it as "the measure or limit of the creature's duration." But then he qualifies the programmatic statement:

> It is not easy to express the true notion of time; it hath not any essence or existence of its own, but is an adjunct, or in some sense a quality that belongs to all second beings. It is

18. CB, pp. 47, 59.

therefore no where to be found by itself, but always adhering
to the thing as its subject.[19]

Temporality is ingredient to the nature of beings that exist
by participation, not some absolute thing that second beings participate in. If there were no creatures, then there
would be no time. The character of time is such that it
has a beginning and end, and a succession that flows: "time
is not a standing, but a moving thing, and it is always in
motion, without any cessation." Consequently, time must
be seen as past, present, and future.

> Time *past* is all the time which the thing hath run through
> since it first had its existence till the point in which it now
> is; it hath past through, and left it behind it. Time *present*
> is the season just before the creature, or that individual mo-
> ment of existence, which is just now in being. Time *to come*
> is that which remains of the allotted duration of it, till the
> last sand be run out, and it shall have no more to do with
> this being or existence. In these respects we say of the crea-
> ture, that yesterday is gone, today is present, tomorrow is to
> come; and we can in no sense bring yesterday and tomorrow
> to commence with today.[20]

All this is true of even those creatures that are immortal.
Angels, for example, once were not.

> There was no world, no creature, no beginning of time be-
> fore these were made. They were made *with* time, not in
> succession of time, and therefore are as ancient as time it-
> self. (Emphasis added.)[21]

Beings by participation, regardless of their position within
the great chain of being, are temporal. Temporality is essential to creaturely existence.

19. CB, p. 59.
20. CB, p. 59.
21. CB, p. 111.

In contradistinction to temporality stands God's eternality. By negating the defining characteristics of time, Willard proceeds through the negative route to an understanding of what eternity is not. God's "duration admits of none of these limitations" of time.

> As there never was a time when he [God] was not, so neither could it ever be said, that he began to be. He is without original; he never was a possible being, but was ever *in act*. He never was in a state of non-being, from whence he was to pass into existence.
>
> There have no times passed over him, but he enjoys himself in an everlasting NOW. . . . He hath in himself a full and perfect possession of everlasting and interminable life, *all at once,* and hath no succession of thoughts, notions, or visions, but drinks up all his felicity at once and eternally.
>
> There never will come a time when his being will cease; but he will be the same after infinite ages.
>
> Eternity admits of no divisions; it is a standing thing. Things fleet in respect of themselves, but in respect to him, he sees them in the same everlasting instant. He looks neither backward nor forward. Things past are present with him, and so are things to come; and therefore, as the notion of present hath regard to succession, it is not compatible to him.[22]

Willard does not claim that any positive knowledge is gained through this negative approach. Indeed, he speaks only to keep from remaining silent: man is "incapable of thinking of eternity, but only under the notion of an infinite time," and yet strictly speaking this is not the literal truth. "I confess," Willard concedes in a moment of candor, "these notions are improper, but they serve to hint something of his eternity to us." [23]

22. CB, p. 59.
23. CB, p. 60.

When it comes to the communicable perfections of wisdom, power, holiness, justice, goodness, and truth, the positive content becomes more specifiable, for traces of these are ascertainable in the created order of this world. Where the metaphysical attributes strip away that which is unworthy of absolute perfection, the moral virtues yield analogous meanings. For example, in discussing the holiness of God, Willard argues in the following manner:

> God is holy originally, the creatures are so by derivation. His Holiness is the prototype, theirs but the copy; his the substance, theirs but the image or shadows; his the fountain, theirs but some few drops, or small springs that issue from it. All the holiness that is in all the creatures is borrowed of him. He hath his in and of himself, and they have theirs of and from him.[24]

In the essential order the prime analogate is in God and is applied analogously to the creature. But in the order of knowing, the process is reversed. The mind begins with the derived perfection as it is known within the creaturely sphere, and then elevates it through the dialectic of the incommunicable qualities so that it becomes worthy of God "in a more sublime and supereminent manner." God is not only good; he is an infinite, eternal, and immutable good—goodness itself.

Because all the attributes in this abstract form are *in* God's essence, they *are* God's essence. In putting it this way Willard denies categorically any independent reality to these perfections. They are God's own being, not some idealized form standing behind or over against the living God. Furthermore, the Infinite does not need the finite; Goodness Itself, being infinite, would suffer no loss at all were there nothing but God. According to Willard, God "hath enough in himself to answer his own ends."

24. CB, p. 73.

He hath no need to fetch in any supply from abroad. He
wanted nothing in those eternal ages, when he was alone,
and there was no being beside him. . . . His infinite will
completely acquiesceth in himself.[25]

The world in no way is essential to God.

Understanding and will in the divine life

Even though God could have remained all alone without
the slightest loss of power or value, Willard's Absolute in
fact is not some cosmic introvert who is content to remain
shut up in some happy estate wherein he enjoys himself
with an "infinite self-love." He who stands in need of
nothing freely moves outside himself to "have a world to
be a mirror of his perfections." If this world is to exist,
then it is necessary for it to be derived through God's creative power, because it could never erupt from nothingness
on its own. Does this entail that the world is derived necessarily from God's nature? If yes, then the world would be
necessary exactly like God, which would be blasphemous.
Willard therefore goes to the contrary, arguing that God's
creative will is "arbitrary." What this means is intelligible
only within the framework of Willard's statements on the
faculties of "understanding" and "will" in the living God.
(Strictly speaking, "there is no faculty in God really distinct
from his essence," but in order to discuss God's wisdom
and power, or knowing and willing, it is necessary to speak
as if God had these faculties.)

God knows and wills, and he does so on three different
levels which are readily distinguishable within Willard's
treatment of the problem. First, in regard to himself, God
knows himself to be goodness itself; therefore he loves himself necessarily. It is impossible for God not to will to be

25. CB, pp. 46–49, 65, 95; cf. 273.

necessitate any creativity at all. But *if* God so decides to work outside himself, then he freely chooses the best in terms of his own glory, not in terms of anything other than himself.[29]

God is free to create or not, and he is not exhausted in his creativity. But God also is faithful. Having determined what is the best means of declaring his glory, the decision is final and irreversible. In choosing to actualize his eternal schema God commits himself to run the course his infinite wisdom has laid out without the slightest deviation. In terms of what the creation is up against in respect to God's power, Willard insists that what is fundamental is not God's *absolute power* (what he is able to do), but rather God's *ordained power* (what he is pleased to do). And God has freely chosen to create and govern this world.

29. CB, pp. 70, 101; cf. 66, 69, 89, 251, 377, 540; SM, p. 19; PIC, p. 11.

CHAPTER FOUR

The Created and Governed World

He never intended to make a world, and then put the government of it out of his own hands, nor yet to lose the liberty of governing of it as he sees meet. He will maintain his authority.[1]

The world that God deliberately and freely actualizes from among the realm of possibilities grounded in the divine essence is a rather extensive hierarchical universe. In ordaining this particular world to stand out in existence, God's works of "efficiency" are manifest for all mankind to behold. This "efficiency," moreover, is disclosed not only in and through the given order of creation which is suspended over "the abyss of nothing"; God's invisible hand providentially guides this same world towards its ordained end. Around the poles of creation and providence Willard organizes his cosmology. Except in one major detail Willard's understanding of the world is informed by the light of nature and is capable of defense, to his own mind at least, by right reason. (The diagrammatic chart opposite is included to facilitate the exposition; it is constructed from Willard's lectures in 1690.)

1. CB, p. 191.

The Order of Creation

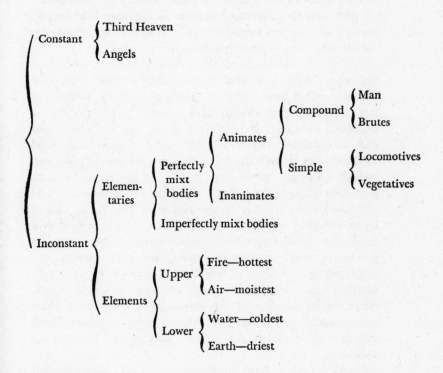

The created order of the world

Willard's most basic distribution of created reality lies between constant and inconstant natures, or to use the biblical language, "heaven and earth." Both sides of this dichotomy fall within created being and therefore are radically distinct from their Maker, but between the inconstant "earth" and the constant "heaven" a decisive difference is present which plays a crucial role in Willard's anthropology, for man by nature participates in both realms.

The visible world and all that resides therein is *inconstant* because it arises out of a "pre-existing matter" that God initially called forth from the abyss of nothing. Originally the inconstant was chaotic and is only "made perfect by degrees"; therefore, it is subject to the law of "generation and corruption." Beginning with some primal stuff, God differentiates it into the four elements of pre-Socratic cosmology (fire, air, water, and earth), with the higher two still "ascending and moving toward the circumference" and the lower two "tending to the center of the world." From these four elements, then, the generating power of God produces the higher forms of the elementaries. The lowest elementaries, such as meteors, snow, and earthquakes, are imperfect in the sense of not being "firm, stable and permanent." But more to the point are those perfectly mixed elementaries which give the world its more durable character. Inanimates of this type consist "only of a body" and lack the spirit of life that joins a soul to the body of all animates.

"Soul" provides every living being in God's creation with "self-motion." Where inanimates move only when they are acted upon by "an adventitious impulse," such as "a principle of gravity and levity," all animates have an "internal principle" of action. The animates, furthermore, are subdivided into simple and compound animates, with the former dichotomized into the vegetatives (the plant kingdom) and the locomotives (the sun and moon and stars, which Willard conceives of as being alive). Compound animates, in addition to vegetative and locomotive souls, also have a "life of sense," that is, they have four "inward senses" (imagination, cogitation, memory, and affections) and five "outward senses." Among all the compound animates, however, man alone has a "reasonable soul . . . endowed with the faculties of understanding and will." And it is through this highest power in man that he is capable of knowing and loving. Without it man would lack freedom; because of it man shares with the angels the higher world of constant natures. (Detailed consideration of Willard's anthropology will be presented in the following chapter.)

The angels who make their abode in the "third heaven" have *constant* natures. Instead of developing by degrees, they were created "perfect in the first moment of time." They were created "with time" and therefore are "as ancient as time itself." And because "their existence was complete from the beginning," they are not bound by the laws of "generation and corruption" as are all inconstant natures. Even though they are "perpetual or aeviternal," they still are creatures. Therefore, "to think them *immaterial* is absurd"; rather, "they have the finest matter." "They are capable of torment; they are not a mere *act*, as God is, but have a protention; they are quantity and not infinite." Carrying the point to its logical conclusion, Willard claims that even the "third heaven" is "made of the most pure and subtle matter of all bodies in the world." [2]

While God could have created Willard's hierarchical

2. CB, pp. 110–21.

universe in "an instant," it in fact pleased him to bring it
into actuality through the more "leisurely" pace of six
days. Reason alone is sufficient to "contemplate the nature,
order and frame of things," but how long God spent in
shaping the cosmos is discoverable only through the Genesis
account, although there is still nothing offensive to reason,
in Willard's opinion, about this temporal progression. And
given the basic schema from Genesis Willard felt free to
add to it. For example, in discussing meteors he casually
asserts that though they are "not named in the history of
the creation, yet [they] are to be understood, as the workmanship of the third day." Natural philosophy or science
still meshed with the biblical account at Harvard in the
late seventeenth century.

At one point, however, Willard moves beyond what he
thinks the finite mind of man can comprehend, namely,
that God created the world *ex nihilo*. In creating this world,
God's activity is unfathomable. What is done is "altogether
new; the thing was nothing before creation gave it a being."
God did not merely shape new things out of some eternal
prime matter, for there is nothing eternal other than God.
Creation is a mystery of the faith to be accepted on authority.

> This article [of creation out of nothing] belongs to the doc-
> trines of faith; and carnal reason knows not how to com-
> prehend it; and therefore the wisdom of heathen philosophy
> was here puzzled and nonplust. Many of them taught the
> works of creation so far, as to acknowledge there was a time
> when there were no particular creatures, nor forms of things,
> neither elementaries, nor any elements; nothing but a rude
> and indigested heap or chaos of formless matter, on which
> they confess the Eternal Agent did work, and out of which
> he educed all the species of beings, giving them their several
> forms and qualities, and appointed them their several ends
> and uses. But still this material principle of the world, they
> thought to be co-eternal with God. The ground of which

opinion was, a maxim taken up in heathen philosophy, *ex nihilo nihil fit,* from whence they concluded it to be an utter impossibility in the thing, that ever any being should be produced from a bare non-entity. But this principle is not universally true. If we consider the ordinary course of nature, or look upon nature as now constituted; now things are not ordinarily made, but are of some pre-existent matter. But if we speak of nature in its constitution, or seek into the first order or condition of beings, there was a supernatural work in that; and though nature cannot, yet the God of nature can, and doth produce something out of nothing; and out of that something, all things.[3]

Interestingly enough, Willard defends this mystery that defies comprehension not so much through biblical authority as through a dialectical reduction to absurdity of any alternative.

This pre-existent matter must be either creature, or the Creator. This is the highest distribution of beings that we can rise unto. And what absurdities are there, which necessarily follow upon either of these suppositions? For,

1. If we suppose it to be the Creator, then we confess it to be God himself; then we make the efficient and the matter to be the same; then God must communicate of his own substance to the creature; then there is in the divine essence a material principle, and that divisible and capable of generation and corruption; and then the creature proceeds from God naturally and not voluntarily, eternally and not in time. All which are blasphemous conclusions, and altogether repugnant to the nature of God.

2. If we suppose it to be a creature, then it must have an original, and thence it must have a time when it began to be, before which it was not; and therefore that matter must ultimately be made of nothing; for to suppose a pre-existent matter of that matter, is not to evade the intricacy, but to

3. CB, pp. 109–10.

make it more entangled. So that of necessity, our contemplation of these things must ultimately resolve itself here, viz.
That all things came firstly out of nothing.[4]

Even though by rational necessity only God could have
created this world in the radical sense of "giving to a thing
its whole and entire being," Willard still maintains that
how this is so "we impotent creatures cannot comprehend";
it is "more than we can think." But once God threw the
hierarchical universe into existence, the mind can contemplate and understand it as it is. The world has relative
solidity, for God "preserves the creature in its existence."
If for one moment God withdrew his sustaining power, the
cosmos would revert back into the "ancient nothing" from
which God called it into existence.[5]

Viewed in and by itself, the cosmos is "shiftless," because
it is infected at the very core of its being with nothingness,
a negative principle. But when it is seen in its "absolute
dependence" upon God, the world which is man's theater
of activity can be counted on to have a recognizable structure. The God who creates, cares: "He would never have
made it, if he had not intended to look after it." And one
way in which God's faithfulness is manifest is through his
sustaining "the *species* of beings" that he originally created:

> He keeps up all the several sorts of beings which he made
> at the first; so as that there is no one of them that ever was,
> but still is in the world; and shall be as long as the world
> stands, notwithstanding all the hazards which some of them
> do run of being utterly extinct.[6]

The solidity of this world rests not upon some intrinsic
power ingredient in created being but upon the constancy
of God's sustaining will.

4. CB, p. 110.
5. CB, pp. 108–10.
6. CB, pp. 130–31, 139–41, 150.

God's providential governance of the world

Not only is the world created and sustained by the sovereign power of God's efficient will; God also oversees the complete unfolding of the divine plan for his workmanship. The cosmic watch, so to speak, is not wound up so perfectly that it can run on its own internal spring of action. That even creatures who "are void of knowledge and understanding" still pursue their proper ends testifies to a governor who "is not an idle spectator, but an agent in all." Unless one is prepared to invest the universe as a whole with an autonomous "soul," as Willard points out some philosophers did, the only way to account for intelligible design is through a transcendent cause: "the soul of the world is divine providence, guiding every thing by the rules of infinite wisdom." Without God's direction the cosmos could not be "rational" and God's end in view would be frustrated.[7]

Given Willard's belief that "the whole world is a sucking infant depending on the breasts of divine providence," it is not surprising that he accepts a deterministic view of God's ordering of the affairs of the universe.

> This common government of God is exercised upon the creatures, by a sovereign predetermination of all actions of it.
>
> This pre-determination overrules, orders, and disposeth of all the actions of second causes at pleasure.
>
> . . . all must issue and resolve into this arbitrary government of God, who acts as a great monarch, who gives not an account of his matters to the children of men, but holds the creatures in a full subordination to his absolute pleasure.[8]

To stop with these quotations, however, would misrepresent Willard's full position rather badly, for in maintaining

7. CB, pp. 130, 136, 146.
8. CB, pp. 147–48.

that God is the "first cause of all things," Willard does not
for a moment deny the instrumentality of "second causes."
Indeed, God's government of the world "respects the actions of the creatures according to their innate principles." [9]
A "co-operation" between the Creator and creature per-
tains in every natural operation. And this "concourse"
works "in and by" the secondary causality that is appropriate to the nature of the given creature. In acting, the
second being follows a "natural principle"—it "acts *naturally* and not *forcedly*."

> God acts efficiently and influentially; the creature acts in-
> strumentally and formally. God acts as the first and supreme
> [cause]; the creature as the second, as a subordinate cause.[10]

In every event God "is always intimately present with the
creature," directing it towards the end for which God created it, but it is genuinely the creature's act, too.[11] As
Willard puts it in his first published sermon (1673), God's
"efficiency is the first mover, he is as it were the first wheel
of the great clock of the world, or the spring of this watch.
Second beings have an operation, but it hath an absolute
dependence upon his co-operation." [12]

To Willard's mind, the most difficult intellectual problem
involved in his position concerns the manner of holding
together the contingency of any given occurrence with the
necessity that grows out of God's willing it to happen.
Given the world, if contingency is denied, then the world
becomes necessary. But if God's act is denied, then the
world is capricious at best, or at worst ceases to be. To cut
through the horns of this dilemma Willard distinguishes
between two types of necessity. First, there is an "absolute"

9. CB, pp. 133, 143.
10. CB, p. 136.
11. CB, p. 134; cf. PPRM, pp. 70–71.
12. UI, p. 24.

or "natural" necessity that "flows from the very nature and being of the thing." With this type nothing could be otherwise than it is. But a second type of necessity functions in a different way. With a "hypothetical" or "conditionate" necessity it is simply requisite that some prior condition be met in order for something to happen. Where natural necessity is grounded in the nature of things, the hypothetical type "flows from the *connexion* of things one with another." [13] And it is with this latter meaning of necessity in mind that Willard attempts to pierce the problem:

> Now this necessity doth not arise from the nature of the thing itself, but from the supposition of something going before, which determines the event, as that, for that reason, it cannot be otherwise. And such a necessity as this is, must be acknowledged to be found, in things which in their own nature, are mutable and contingent. Nor doth this necessity alter the nature of the thing itself, but only gives us reason to conclude of the event, that it shall certainly be so. This is usually called necessity of infallibility; and from hence we argue that if God hath purposed a thing to be, it shall not be frustrated, because his purposes are unchangeable. But this purpose doth not, itself, alter the nature of the thing, nor obstruct its natural acting, nor lay any compulsion upon it.[14]

God's presence does not remove the natural power at all; rather God's efficient first act makes the natural or second act possible.

Over and beyond God's "ordinary" way of exercizing his efficiency within the world, Willard leaves room for miracles or "extraordinary" providences in which God skips over "the order of the natural course of things"—that is, both the first and second act are God's. The total effect of Willard's treatment of the miraculous, however, is such

13. CR, p. 65; cf. CB, p. 377.
14. BRGK, p. 10.

that its importance is minimal.[15] The dominant line of
argument is overwhelmingly under the hegemony of a
metaphysical concern for the laws of nature and nature's
God who governs all things to accomplish the plan he freely
chose when the very foundation of the world was estab- .
lished. And given this metaphysical posture, the burning
issue centers in human freedom and the fact of moral evil.

15. CB, p. 138; cf. RDPT, p. 6.

CHAPTER FIVE

Man the Reasonable Creature

See what an excellent being man was as he came out of the hands of his Creator. He must be a rare piece of workmanship, about whose making God should call a counsel and enter into deliberation. God made all things in wondrous wisdom; but here was a result of all God's creating wisdom gathered together in one. There were many beams of his wisdom, power and goodness scattered among other creatures; here they are all contracted in this little model.[1]

Man's natural endowment: body and soul

Of all the inhabitants of the vast world God so exuberantly creates, sustains, and governs for his own glory, man is the most "excellent," for what God "scattered among other creatures" is "contracted in this little model" in such a way that man is a microcosm reflecting the entire multitudinous universe. Each level in the great chain of being, according to Willard, is represented in man's natural endowment: "the four elements" are represented in his body (rocks), the power to grow is represented in his vegetable soul (plants), the power to move is represented in his locomotive soul (stars), the powers to perceive, think, remem-

1. CB, p. 122.

ber, and feel are represented in his sensitive soul (animals), and the powers to know, judge, and choose are represented in his rational soul (angels). The following diagrammatic schema exhibits Willard's conception of how each ascending stage integrates the lower into a higher synthesis of capability.

As the only being who spans the cosmological divide between the visible, inconstant world and the invisible, constant realm, man is unique because he stands at the juncture of earth and heaven, nature and spirit. That is his place, according to Willard, and no man can snuff out

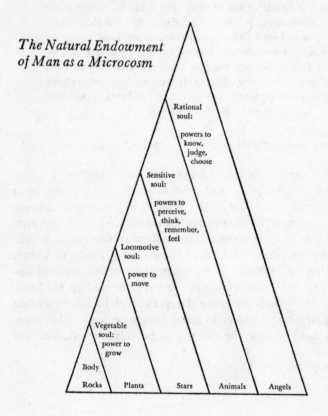

The Natural Endowment of Man as a Microcosm

Rational soul:

powers to know, judge, choose

Sensitive soul:

powers to perceive, think, remember, feel

Locomotive soul:

power to move

Vegetable soul: power to grow

Body

Rocks   Plants   Stars   Animals   Angels

his inner awareness of this special position in God's creation with all that it entails for human destiny.[2]

The distinctive place man holds in the hierarchical order of the universe determines Willard's fundamental anthropological doctrine: "Man consists of two essential constituting parts, viz. a body, and a reasonable soul. Neither of these alone is the man, but both in conjunction. . . . both go together to his specifications and personality."[3] With his body man is rooted in the inconstant world of terrestrial beings; with his reasonable soul man shares with the angels the celestial sphere of constant natures. Both are constitutive of his natural endowment; both are "essential to his humanity."

Because of his "bodily and sensible part," Willard's man "participates in the same genus with his fellow animals, being a living creature with a compound life."[4] What this means, in the first instance, is that man's body is not essentially different from that of animals. In the second instance, it means that man shares fully the life of animals, and according to Willard animals live on three discernible levels. First, animals have the same "quickening spirit" that characterizes plants, namely, "a vegetative life" by which they grow. Second, animals have a "motive soul" or "a power of self-motion." What specifically makes this individual being an animal, however, is the third level of life, that is, "a life of sense." This latter power enables an animal to perceive "sensible objects, by its bodily organs":

> There must be an object for them; for the acts of the senses terminates on something without them. It is something which is presented before them, for them to act upon, which object meets with the sensitive spirit in the organ, by which the object is represented unto, and made present with it.[5]

2. CB, p. 127.
3. CB, pp. 231, 528; cf. 296–300; SM, p. 9.
4. CB, p. 122.
5. CB, p. 119.

Perception or sensation of any exterior object over against the animal is made through the five "outward senses" (touch, taste, smell, hearing, and sight). Beyond these Willard also includes the four "inward senses":

1. The imagination or the fancy; which takes in the images of things, and receives the impression of them, as they are brought in by the outward senses. It is as it were the porter, which takes in the species of things, as they are offered unto it.

2. The cogitation; which lays together and composeth the things which are presented unto the fancy, whereby the sensitive creature as it were, doth conclude sensibly; and accordingly either embraceth, or avoids the object; and by this the creature is capable of forming other objects; from whence sensitive creatures are capable of dreaming, which is nothing but the working of the cogitation.

3. The memory; whereby the creature is able to lay up, what cogitation hath laid together; and to bring them together again unto the fancy, when there is occasion. And by this the sensible creature, having formerly seen an object and observed it, knows it upon sight a great while after.

4. The affections; which are nothing else but the reflection of cogitation upon the heart, by which it is moved according to the impression it had there made. And by virtue hereof are sensitive beings variously affected with love, hatred, fear, desire, etc. And these appear in some of them unto admiration.[6]

This "sensitive soul," which man shares with all the animals, sleeps, and in so doing "binds up the external senses from acting." [7]

Unambiguously and consistently maintained is the funda-

6. CB, p. 120.
7. CB, p. 120.

mental conviction that everything ingredient to the nature
of brute animals is an essential dimension of man's natural
endowment. Insofar as man functions on this lower level
he is guided by instinct and only passively reflects the glory
of God. That which opens the peculiarly human arena,
however, is "the reasonable soul" added to the inconstant
nature man receives from the lower echelons in the great
chain of being. This higher power carries man into the
invisible, constant world, the abode of angels. Through the
reasonable soul human beings are "fitted for being *active*
instruments in serving God, their Maker, and in their natures capacitated for the discharge of this high and glorious
service." [8] (Emphasis added.) Standing at the juncture of
nature and spirit, with, so to speak, a foot in both worlds,
man is essentially and irrevocably bound to the invisible
world as well as to the visible.

Even though Willard argues that the "reasonable soul"
is a "spiritual substance," this should not be construed in
such a way as to negate the soul's *materiality*. That spiritual
substances are nonetheless material is unequivocally maintained by Willard:

> It [the rational soul] hath least matter and most form. It is
> materiated, or else it would not stand separated without a
> miracle. There is no pure act or form standing alone, that
> being a property incommunicable of the first being. It hath
> the properties of a spirit in it. It is most active; it has a kind
> of ubiquity; it is from one end of the earth to another in a
> little time; it is never out of action; it sleeps not in or with
> the body; that is at work when the senses are bound up; it
> is of wondrous strength. Men can kill the body, but not
> annihilate the soul.[9]

Simply to exist in either the inconstant, visible realm or
the constant, invisible realm requires materiality, for to

8. CB, p. 121.
9. CB, p. 123.

deny materiality to spiritual substance would be "to ascribe
an absolute deity to them." It should be registered at this
point, however, that "matter" is being used here in the
Aristotelian sense of "potentiality," not in the common-
sensical meaning of "corporeality." The gulf between earth
and heaven, or the inconstant and constant worlds, is a
division within the larger genus of finite beings and in no
way should that dichotomy be confused with the primal
dichotomy between increated and created being. The Creator alone exists without matter or potentiality, that is,
God is Pure Act. In terms of materiality the difference between the Creator and creatures of all levels is absolute,
but between constant and inconstant creatures this difference is only one of degree. The decisive, defining difference
here lies not with "matter" at all, but rather in the fact
that only spiritual substances are *immortal*, or negatively
put, they are not subject to the natural law of generation
and corruption, and consequently are "capable of no other
dissolution, but annihilation, which shall never be." [10] The
diagram shown opposite sorts out Willard's programmatic
distinctions.

By asserting that the reasonable soul is a "spiritual substance," Willard commits himself to the position that it is
a distinct entity "capable of existing and acting in a state
of separation" from the body. "The soul being a constant
nature, remains entire and active, and no whit impaired in
its natural powers by being separate." Indeed, the soul
"doth many things by itself, without the help of the body,
while in it, which prove it able to act without the aid of
this instrument." Because of the essential difference between
the nature of body and soul, Willard concludes that each
is created by God in a "different manner." [11] One's body is
propagated through the sexual act, but not so one's rational

10. CB, p. 123; cf. pp. 195, 227, 529, 560; IS, p. 37.
11. CB, pp. 231, 233, 529.

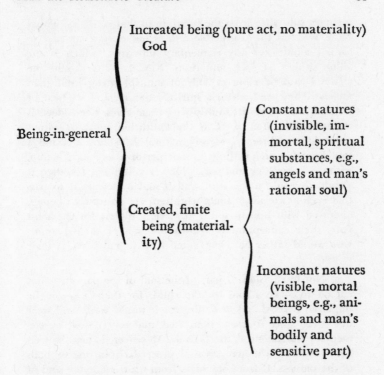

Increated being (pure act, no materiality) God

Being-in-general

Created, finite being (materiality)

Constant natures (invisible, immortal, spiritual substances, e.g., angels and man's rational soul)

Inconstant natures (visible, mortal beings, e.g., animals and man's bodily and sensitive part)

soul. "The soul is not traduced or derived from the parents, but is immediately created by God himself." Willard's argumentation on this particular doctrine (traditionally known as "Creationism") deserves quotation in full, for it is one of his most extensive uses of a negative reduction.

If the soul be propagated, it is either by multiplication, division, or seminal generation. I know not a fourth way that can be concerned; and therefore the disjunction is full.

Now,

1. It is not by multiplication. Some say one soul multiplies another, as one light lights up another. But the comparison will not hold. For, 1. There is a communication of an ele-

mentary substance from the lighting, to that which is lighted
by it, whereas the reasonable soul is not elementary and so
cannot administer any elementary substance, which is the
alone subject of such mutations. Nay, 2. Why should the
rational soul be more capable of multiplicating itself than
angels? They are both of a spiritual nature, and we hear of
no such way of spirits multiplying themselves, nor indeed is
it intelligible. Yea, 3. This multiplication must be either
natural, or voluntary. Merely natural it is not, because a
soul knowing and willing, cannot perform any such action,
without knowledge and will. Nor yet voluntary, for then it
should depend on the will. And if so, how comes it to pass
that such as are illegitimate [children] are reasonable beings,
endowed with human souls? It is certain that for the most
part, their conception is against the will of their parents,
who would rather have prevented it, if it had been in their
power.

2. Not by division. A part of the soul of the parents is not
cut off to make a soul for the child; for then it would be
impaired hereby, and so by degrees it would waste and wear
out itself, since it is not nourished, and so repaired by elementary nutriment as the body is. Moreover, it may be well
here inquired whether this soul proceeds from one or both
of the parents. If from one only, from which? For the soul of
each is equally divisible? If from both equally, how comes a
soul which is without parts, to be made up of several parts?

3. Not by seminal generation. For the soul is an immortal
and constant being, and is not therefore a subject of generation. Whatsoever is produced by generation, is in its own
nature liable to corruption. But this is contrary to the nature
of the reasonable soul which was made incorruptible. We
shall therefore find the different manner of the creation of
the body, and of the soul.[12]

The soul is either created immediately by God, or it is
derived from parents by either multiplication, or division,

12. CB, pp. 194–95.

or seminal generation; not from parents by any conceivable process; therefore, from God immediately, and in turn this secures the soul's essential difference from the body, for the body is propagated sexually from parents.

Although every immortal soul is created immediately by God as a separate spiritual substance, and consequently is not subject to the natural law of generation and decay, Willard still maintains that *man is mortal*. By itself the soul is not a man. To be human is to be embodied, that is, a man is a composite being joining together in "one complete subsistence" an inconstant body and a constant soul. This union is effected through "the animal and vital spirits" which form the point of contact between the two disparate substances. Because this union is produced by the lower part, the union itself is subject to generation and corruption.

> The soul and body are thus united together by generation. By which union they become one person. This union is that in which generation properly results. The whole body, animal and vital spirits, which are the bond of this union, are produced by this generation. And by virtue of this operation, the body is fashioned and organized, the soul is received into union, and so one complete subsistence is made.
>
> . . . as man's body was made of dissoluble principles, being elementary, so the bond of union by which that [body] and the soul were conjoined was dissoluble; this bond was the vital spirits, which were the soul's vehicle, and tied it to the body, and therefore by the extinction of those spirits, the separation comes to be made.[13]

During this earthly life the body and soul are "two dear companions," and the soul has "a love to, and inclination to continue in union with that body and though sickness, pain, and trouble render it a troublesome lodging, yet had

13. CB, pp. 195, 231, 233.

it [the soul] rather abide in it, under great inconveniences, than be dislodged." But when death dissolves the union, even though the soul continues to exist in separation, this particular man forthwith ceases to exist. "A soul and a body are both essential to humanity, nor can a being be truly called man, that doth not consist of both." [14]

A cause by counsel: understanding and will

Although both body and soul are of "the essence of humanity" and neither is separable from human nature as such, it is man's immortal soul alone that provides him with his distinctive character and differentiates him from the brutes. The rational soul is what makes man "a moral agent," "a rational agent," "a free and voluntary agent," or as Willard more frequently refers to the active, personal self, "a cause by counsel." [15] As such an agent man holds out before himself a project to shape his life, to give it meaning and value.

Man can both propound to himself his own end, and make choice of the means or way leading unto it. He can deliberate with himself about these things, and take that which likes himself, and leave that which is not grateful unto him. None [and this includes God] can either compel or hinder him in his choice, but he can follow the dictates of his own understanding. From whence it follows, that all his human actions are voluntary and deliberate.[16]

Unless the interiority of human consciousness is to be written off as sheer illusion, man is equipped with the ability

14. CB, pp. 123–25, 528, 536, 541; MW, p. 13; cf. MRL, p. 8; SM, p. 9; PT, p. 29.
15. CB, pp. 195, 209, 214, 443, 528; BRGK, p. 45; MM, p. 93; CE, p. 87.
16. CB, p. 124.

to make a "rational and deliberate choice." [17] To strip him of this would reduce him to a sub-human level and render moral accountability superfluous.

In order to understand what "a voluntary agent" means for Willard, it is necessary to juxtapose it to "a natural agent" within the more inclusive class of agents as such.

> In every agent we consider a power which is in it, and that seated in the faculties, and is in them a principle of operation, which is called the habit, and is that whereby it is fitted to serve to its end. And there is such a power in every faculty, and that various, according to the end and use of it. . . . Now whensoever this power is exerted by any faculty in the creature, that is properly an action, and that is always by applying to an object.[18]

An agent is that which has within itself the power to act. This power is correlative to the object, the end in view. Whenever this capability is exercised, there is an action. Now if any action originates instinctually, then the agent lacks the capacity to choose; it must act in response to the object; therefore the action is natural. If the highest level of action of which any given agent is capable is only natural action, then that agent is "a natural agent." But if and when "rational and spontaneous" action is exhibited, then the agent of such action obviously is capable of activities that transcend natural actions, and this capability is rooted in higher levels that make any agent who can exert such power a "voluntary agent," and such is man.

In maintaining that man is a voluntary agent, Willard does not deny that man also functions on the natural levels, for the "bodily and sensible part" of his natural endowment requires man to respond *on the levels appropriate,*

17. CB, p. 214.
18. CB, p. 212; cf. pp. 144ff.

like an animal. But man's *humanity* is not disclosed there. His humanity depends on his ability to take thought, choose freely, and exercise self-determination. Not every action a man in fact takes is voluntary, but "all his *human* actions are voluntary and deliberate." [19]

From the deliberate and voluntary character of "human actions," Willard concludes that man's reasonable soul must have at least two distinct but inseparable faculties, namely, understanding and will.

> The nature of a creature is those powers and principles which are put into it, whereby it is rendered capable of acting in its own orb. The nature then of a reasonable creature, as such, is that power which it had given it to act as a moral agent under a rule: and that is an ability of knowing, and electing, or choosing and refusing. Its actions are such things as it doth by the exertion of that nature, or principle which is in it; or whatsoever it doth under the influence of its reason and will.[20]

That knowing and choosing are two distinct operations in the soul, Willard makes unmistakably clear:

> It is one thing to declare that we find a thing to be thus and so, and another thing to pass an act thereupon, in either choosing or refusing the thing according as it is so found. And though this latter is built upon the former, yet it is another thing quite different from it.

> Hence, they infer two diverse powers in the soul to exert them. As passing a judgment on a thing, and passing an act of choice or refusal, are in themselves vastly different, so we must conceive the power of exerting them to be as different; so that they must flow from two principles, really diverse one from another. As without knowledge there can be no judgment past, so without liberty, there can no election be made.

19. CB, p. 149.
20. CB, p. 209; cf. TBM, p. 293.

Now reason tells us, that knowledge is one thing, and liberty another.

That the former of these is that which we call understanding, and the latter the will. Which, though they belong to one and the same soul, yet are several powers of it, and accordingly are generally supposed to be distinct faculties. However [moreover?], the Word of God every where speaks of them distinctly, and assigns these actions accordingly to them. That whereby we discern things, and give in our verdict about them, is called the understanding. That whereby we determine on our object, and resolve upon our actions, we call the will.[21]

In "passing a judgment" the mind transcends the power of "cogitation" in the sensitive soul and rises to the sphere of truth. The move made here by Willard needs to be considered with care, for understanding or reason ranges across being in ways that leave mere cogitation groveling in empirical dust. It will be recalled that the *sensitive* soul contains the inward sense of *cogitation,* and this power was cryptically described as that faculty which

lays together and composeth the things which are presented unto the fancy, whereby the sensitive creature as it were, doth conclude sensibly; and accordingly either embraceth, or avoids the object. And by this the creature is capable of forming other objects; from whence sensitive creatures are capable of dreaming, which is nothing but the working of the cogitation.[22]

The sensitive soul which man shares with animals is equipped to abstract the "effigy" of the external thing and bring it into focus as an object of consciousness. What is presented at this level is strictly limited to that which is empirically or "sensibly" derivable, namely, matters of fact

21. CB, p. 454.
22. CB, p. 120.

or states of affairs. Even though by cogitation man may re-arrange these different perceptions into more complex patterns, these can be traced to their origin in sensible experience. What cogitation can never do is penetrate through to the *being* of the thing in itself—cogitation is saddled with appearance. It cannot form "an axiom, sentence, assertion, or negation about" the objects of experience. It cannot interrogate reality. It is not in a position to form a judgment concerning the "truth in the things that be." That prerogative falls under the dominion of the higher power of reason or understanding "which is the only subject of truth." [23] In short, the difference between cogitation and understanding is a difference in *kind,* not *degree,* for the power of his understanding carries man into the area where he can bid for truth.

Truth, in the first instance, "consists in the reality of the thing; if the thing *be,* it is true, and all that wherein it discovers itself to *be;* and to be such a thing, and no other, is from the truth of it." Furthermore, this "metaphysical truth" is anchored in God as the ground of all beings other than the self-sufficient first cause:

> Truth . . . is firstly in him [God], and in them [creatures] only derivatively. The eternal idea which God had in his own infinite understanding, of all things that were to be in time, and all the several managements of them, is the exemplary truth. That which they have in themselves [i.e., metaphysical truth], is but a copy of this. Truth in the creature being its conformity unto that idea which God had of it in himself.[24]

Because metaphysical truth "in the thing itself" is a copy of the exemplary truth in the divine mind, it has objectivity independently of the knowing subject: "it is so

23. CP, p. 75; HM, p. 18; cf. CB, p. 123.
24. HM, p. 8.

whether the understanding do rightly resent it or no." But the mind is naturally at home with reality, for the "proper and suitable object of the understanding is truth, in the search and contemplation whereof it is employed, and when it is so employed, it is about its own work." [25]

The cognitive task is to get the conception formed in the human mind matched to the objective, self-evidencing metaphysical truth in the thing itself. If "nothing at all" is known about the composition or relations of the object, then we are left in total ignorance. If we know something about the object, yet the conception does not correspond to the objective truth, then we fall into error. "Logical truth" is in the understanding only "when the mind takes up a right conception of the thing as it is, and is not mistaken about it." Such a conception comes about by putting together the simple truths "according to the natural and genuine relation they have each to the other so as to make them into a true conclusion." This putting together is an act of "judgment," and Willard believes judgments are divided into two basic types.

First, there is "opinion," which results from "reasons which are only probable and contingent." Even though "some rational connexion" holds between "only probable and conjectural antecedents and consequents," this connection is tied by "a slip knot." For example, "when we say it will be a fair day for the evening is red, though this be an ordinary symptom, yet it is no infallabile presage; it is oftentimes so, and sometimes otherwayes."

In counterdistinction to "opinion" stands "science or knowledge," in which the connections "flow from the very nature of the things, and are therefore necessarily predicated of the subject, and it cannot be without them." "When we discover, and conclude of necessary causes from

25. CB, p. 722.

necessary effects," then our judgment is "tied of a fast knot" and will not slip. Through "an assimilation between the knower, and the thing known," the mind grasps "the whole latitude" of the known object's "real essence." Indeed, because there is a "perfect equality" between the "idea" within the mind and the extra-mental reality apprehended in the cognitive act, "the whole object is so contained in the mind, that nothing, in the thing comprehended, is beyond its knowledge." [26]

Knowing something, however, is quite different from choosing or refusing it, and this latter operation is exerted by a distinct faculty in the reasonable soul—the will. Willard's most fundamental conviction in regard to the will is very simply stated: "The will was made for goodness." [27]

> Now it is the good or evil that is apprehended to be in the object, which do properly come under man's consideration and deliberation, in order to the will's exerting of itself, which hath a natural propensity to choose that which is represented to it as good, and refuse that which it is persuaded to account evil.[28]

The act of choosing good or refusing evil is "performed inwardly by it [the will], and belongs to the sovereignty of the will in the man, by virtue whereof he is a free agent." Technically, such an act of choice is an "elicit act." [29] This should not be taken to mean, however, that the will takes precedence over the understanding in human actions. Quite the contrary is the case simply because the will is dependent upon the judgment of the understanding which evaluates the object.

26. CP, pp. 76–78; cf. CB, pp. 41, 91, 108, 119, 120.
27. CB, p. 534; TBM, p. 424.
28. CB, p. 512.
29. CB, p. 454; cf. p. 185.

> When therefore the understanding hath made inquiry into the nature of an object, and considered what it is in itself, and what respect it hath to the man, it thereupon passeth a judgment, according to the resentment it hath of it, and brings in a verdict in which it declares it to be either good or evil. . . . The goodness that is commended, is that which moves the will to make a choice of it; whereas if it be reported to be evil, that engageth the will to reject it.[30]

In choosing, the will naturally elects the good, and this is its own immediate act, but it chooses *in light of the understanding's value-judgment.* Because this is such a vital issue, the following rather lengthy series of quotations is arranged chronologically in order to exhibit the constancy and consistency of Willard's belief.

> Choice is a judicious and voluntary act, it is a cause by counsel, acting according to the dictates of right reason, and freely resting in the conclusion. (1680)[31]

> . . . every choice ariseth from a rational and convincing discovery of the suitableness of the object chosen, and preference which it is conceived to deserve above others. Now this discovery is made to the understanding, which is the eye of the mind whereby it seeth and judgeth of things. (1684)[32]

> Now a voluntary action is the action of a reasonable creature applying himself to his object, not upon compulsion, nor by the force of instinct, but by the inclination of his own mind; so that as he doth it willingly, he also (and therefore) doth it rationally, or upon some apprehended grounds. (1684)[33]

> Now the natural motion of the will in man, is by the light of the understanding, which is to be eyes unto it. (1686)[34]

30. CB, p. 512.
31. DP, p. 5.
32. MM, p. 149.
33. MM, p. 176.
34. DJ, p. 86.

The act of the will cannot be called an human act, any further than as it follows the dictates and directions of the understanding. (1697)[35]

We are so drawn, that we follow voluntarily, and not by force, or unaccountable instinct. . . . And that we may do it voluntarily, we must do it knowingly; or our understanding must be eyes to our will, and entertain the reason for our so doing. (1698)[36]

Man is a reasonable creature, and his will is one faculty put into him as such a creature; and so it acts according to the influence of the understanding on it; else it were not a human will. (1701)[37]

All human actions are deliberate, in which the understanding is employed, and the will is determined according to the verdict of it. There must therefore be some motive to invite and excite the man to consent, in order to his being prevailed upon. Now the will of man naturally chooseth good, and refuseth evil, according as it is resented by his understanding, which therefore must have such a resentment in order to its commending of it as such. (1701)[38]

After the will has freely decided upon an object, the executive power issues commands to mobilize the entire organism to relate appropriately to the object. These commands are technically called "imperate acts": "The imperate acts of the will are those by which it puts its elections in execution, and pursues them to effect." In this sense, Willard argues, "the will is the regent in man, and the first mover to every action." When the will turns towards an object, the inner man or heart is committed, and the "whole man" follows.[39]

35. CB, p. 437.
36. CB, p. 443.
37. BRGK, p. 15.
38. CE, p. 17.
39. MM, pp. 157, 203; CB, pp. 455, 562.

Human actions: the affections and the body

When the will resolutely makes a deliberate choice, the command center issues an order that is transmitted to the body by the affections, which are "the instruments of the will," "the handmaids of the will," or "the feet of the soul." [40] It is the business of the affections to "carry the man *to* the object that is chosen, and *from* that which is refused. Hence the affections are of two sorts, viz. the closing, and the separating." Basically, love is the closing affection, while hatred is the alienating affection. Under each basic type are sub-types. Willard's comments on love merit quotation in full:

> Now those [derivative affections] that do simply derive from love are three, viz. desire, hope and joy: all of these are but the several effects of love, and all the difference between them ariseth from the diverse site of the object, or respect which it bears unto the will. If the object be represented as good, and the will hath made choice of it, it is to be considered either as absent, and not yet enjoyed, or as in hand and possessed. Now the absence of it doth alone cause this love to exert itself, in an eager longing to be possessed of it, which stimulate the man to pursue it with endeavors, and this is desire. And when together with the absence of the object, there is an apprehended probability or possibility of obtaining it, this prompts and encourageth to a cheerful use of the means, and is hope. But when it hath gotten possession of it, it is in hand, and actually enjoyed, the will acts upon it with delight, and this is properly joy, which ariseth from enjoyment.[41]

The affections set the body in motion to gain or repel the object. "The body is the soul's organ, and it is to perform

40. TBM, p. 470; CB, pp. 211, 455, 582; MM, pp. 298f.
41. CB, p. 512; cf. p. 744; LP, p. 9.

its imperate acts in and with it." [42] Through the body man participates in a world, a human, public world. As a system the body obeys the directions from the control center, and it is through this system that the whole man expresses himself, pursues his ends, pledges his love. Man reaches out towards the end in view, and when the goal is gained, there is a closure of the faculty with the beloved object, and the desire is satisfied.

The pursuit of happiness

As a purposive agent, man organizes the intermediate ends of his life into a coherent pattern of meaning and value around a final or chief end which he believes will satisfy the needs of his own essential being. From the interior, subjective side, the struggle to realize the envisaged good is read by Willard as the "pursuit of happiness." A man can no more evade this pursuit than he can climb out of his own skin or lay aside his self-awareness. By nature man is so "insatiably desirous of happiness" that absolutely nothing can sever him from this "congenerate principle of human nature." [43] Obviously he may fail in his pursuit, but he cannot surrender the quest.

According to Willard, "the nature of a creature is those powers and principles which are put into it, whereby it is rendered capable of acting in its own orb." [44] The "orb" in which man must work out his destiny is one that opens out towards God. Among all the terrestrial creatures, man alone is a free, moral, and rational agent who "grasps after eternity" and has "a natural apprehension of, and desire after immortality." "Brutes have no such thoughts, nor do they

42. PT, p. 140.
43. SD, p. 69; cf. CB, pp. 30, 182, 216, 559, 583, 716, 744.
44. CB, p. 209.

see beyond time." [45] Because "man's soul is of an intellectual nature, and its happiness is suited to a rational being," intrinsic in man's natural, constitutive being is an unquenchable thirst for an infinite good to fulfill his life: "But till all the reachings of the soul are gratified, till all its appetites are filled, it cannot rest; it will be in motion as long as it feels any want." [46]

Man's natural endowment equips him for this exalted position. Regardless of how any given man's actual, historical destiny is worked out, there remains permanently fixed an essential human nature that is common to all persons, whether they are in the religious states of integrity, apostasy, grace, or glory. As long as a man has breath nothing can remove this nature; that which is "essential to his humanity" because it stems "from the principles of nature" is "inseparable" from human nature as such. When Willard addresses man as "a reasonable creature" he is concerned with man's essential being, and it is precisely this microcosm which he sees as "a rare piece of workmanship" in which is "gathered together in one" the full sweep of "God's creating wisdom." [47]

45. CB, pp. 122, 560.
46. CP, pp. 137–38; EP, p. 207; CB, pp. 8, 54, 113, 570.
47. MW, p. 13; CB, pp. 122, 125.

CHAPTER SIX

The Natural Moral Law

*Man was made for an end, viz. to glorify God; and in
subordination thereto, to seek and obtain blessedness.
Now where there is an end propounded, there must
be a way to obtain it; and that which directs to this
way, is the rule; and when it is a proper way to it, it
is then accommodated to the design. Such was the
moral law. And for this reason it is called the moral
law, because it is fitted for the regulating of man in all
the actions of his will, both elicit and imperate. And
by his obedience to it, he should have attained everlasting felicity. Man had a natural craving after happiness, and this was a way to have brought him to it.[1]*

The proper end of human being

As a reasonable creature who deliberately chooses and
freely moves towards his chief end, man inescapably is set
upon some course of action. He cannot stop, he cannot
remain uncommitted, his will cannot remain neutral, for
he is a rational, moral agent who must bid for his fulfillment. The critical question concerns what final end is
sufficient to meet the needs of the human heart for an infinite good. This is a normative question which no manner

1. CB, p. 566.

or amount of sociological investigation is even in a position to address: what "the most of men do *practically* make their end, or propound to themselves as their design" is beside the point.[2] Willard is concerned rather with tracking down the *proper* end of human nature as such, and this is a philosophical quest.

Granted the dynamics of the interior human drive for a final end that will gratify "all the reachings of the soul" and fill "all its appetites," Willard turns to consider what is capable of satisfying a reasonable creature.[3] Obviously the answer must be found within reality, and for analytical purposes the whole system of being in general may be broken down provisionally into three different spheres: (1) the world, (2) man himself, and (3) God.

The world cannot be man's proper end, for then that which is inferior to man in the great chain of being would be acknowledged as superior, or that which serves man would then be his master. But even more fundamentally, the lower creatures "cannot satisfy him."

> The reaches of man's soul are so vast, that they can grasp in the whole creation, and scarce feel it. The desire of man, that horseleeches daughter, is still crying give, give. The bed is too narrow, and the covering too short. The world looks bulky, but it is empty, void and waste. Many have had too much, but never yet any had enough, so as to be content, that had nothing but the creature.[4]

To drink from the fountain of the world as if it were the source of man's ultimate well-being is folly born of ignorance of the deepest needs of human nature.

Man himself, the second alternative, fails the test too, for he knows in his bones that he is a dependent creature

2. CB, p. 2.
3. CP, pp. 137–38; EP, p. 207; CB, pp. 8, 54, 113, 570.
4. CB, p. 608; cf. p. 110.

who lacks self-sufficiency; therefore, "he cannot dwell at home." [5] Man's very quest testifies that the realization of human nature must lie outside himself, and his infinite longing points beyond the created world towards the Transcendent One.

In a nutshell, if man is to be fulfilled, then his felicity must derive from the world, or man, or God; it does not come from either the world or man; therefore, because it is senseless to conceive of man as having natural desires that can not possibly be met, "it follows of necessity" that "God alone is an adequate object for felicity." [6] If man lacked a final destiny that could fulfill his very nature, then life would be an absurd game in which man remained "an everlasting seeker, wandering in his endless quest." "Such an end there must be, or man . . . could never come to his resting place, but must be left in a labyrinth, and carried on in an endless pursuit of happiness." [7] Through an analysis of the human condition Willard concludes that God is the only conceivable proper end of human being, for God alone is able to provide man with the fruition his nature demands. By nature man has a supernatural vocation to enjoy "communion with God" who "is the only objective happiness of the reasonable creature." [8]

The moral law as unchangeable rule

The most fundamental point in Willard's understanding of the moral law is that it is the "rule" by which man ought to conduct the "pursuit of his great end." Where brutes blindly move towards the various ends for which they were created, man is called upon "to pursue his deliberate

5. FO, p. 19; CB, p. 8; MM, p. 88; cf. SM, p. 9.
6. CB, p. 7; cf. CP, p. 138; CB, pp. 110, 128.
7. CB, pp. 2, 3, 6.
8. SM, p. 10; TS, p. 3; cf. CB, pp. 2, 72, 216.

choice" voluntarily. And the moral law is there first to direct man towards his proper end "by showing what is right and what is wrong," and second to be the standard by which his actions are judged to be fitting or not.[9]

As the rule of life the moral law never changes. Regardless of how drastically man warps his being, regardless of how wonderfully God lifts up the most destitute pervert, the moral law continues in unalterable permanence, perpetually established as all mankind's "everlasting rule." Absolutely nothing will render it null and void. The moral law forms the bedrock of all human affairs; man is obligated to it "so long as the natural order of beings abides." [10]

The permanence of the moral law comes directly from the fact that it expresses God's "revealed will" for humankind. At this point a global misunderstanding of Willard's intention may easily occur, for the "revealed will" of God, at first blush, especially in some cryptic passages, seems to be no more than what is revealed in the Bible, with no grounding in human nature. If it is read this way, Willard's thought is badly misconstrued. To put it right will require some patience.

The initial point is that the Bible does contain the revealed will of God in its entirety. Nothing that is needed to light man's path to his final end is lacking there. The Bible fully discloses God's *positive law*. This divine positive law, however, is made up of three distinct types of laws: ceremonial, judicial, and moral laws. One essential difference between the moral law and the other two types is in the temporal extent of their obligation. While the moral law is from everlasting to everlasting, ceremonial and judicial laws are historically conditioned, transient,

9. CB, pp. 560–65; cf. pp. 177, 284.
10. MRL, p. 7; CB, pp. 150, 381, 560, 565, 567; EP, pp. 188f.

and in fact go through significant alterations. For example, the Old Testament law concerning circumcision is no longer binding on Christian consciences; prior to the New Testament dispensation there was no law concerning baptism. It is different with the moral law, which received its classic statement in the Ten Commandments, the positive re-publication of the natural moral law that is written into the very being of man.

> The new edition of the moral law upon Mount Sinai, drawn up into Ten Commandments, was nothing else but a transcript of the [moral] law given to Adam at first.
>
> . . . the Decalogue is an epitome of the whole moral law.[11]

For all the world Moses appears not as a prophet so much as the recording secretary for the celestial court overseeing the eternal moral order of the universe. The one exception to this equivalency of the Ten Commandments and the natural moral law is instructive. The commandment "Remember the Sabbath day and keep it holy" is mixed in character, touching upon both moral and ceremonial matters. That man is morally obligated to worship his Creator has been binding on human consciences ever since the first moment man appeared in creation. But the ceremonial stipulation that he should worship God on the seventh day had to be revealed positively, and it can be altered, and in fact it was changed to the first day of the week after the resurrection of Jesus. The upshot of this discussion is that the moral law positively recorded in the Bible is also *natural*. The acid test for distinguishing between natural and non-natural laws lies not in whether they are positively promulgated, but rather in whether they are *eternally* obligatory. Or to make the same point in another way, the natural moral law cuts across all four

11. CB, p. 150.

religious states—integrity, apostasy, grace, and glory. It addresses "man as man." [12]

Willard's concern here is exclusively with the eternal moral law; that it is also positive does not detract in any way whatever from its fully natural character. It should be mentioned, however, that in putting it this strongly Willard does not in the slightest degree downgrade the positive laws, as will be seen when their content is discussed in the appropriate chapters below.

If the moral law is given to man, as a rational and voluntary agent, to direct all his human actions and is forever obligatory on his conscience, then it must be more than a merely external standard of right and wrong imposed upon him from on high. Duty arises from within, interior to human consciousness, for the natural moral law is "accommodated to the human nature, being every way suited to his frame and constitution." As a standing law it is "engraven on the heart of man at the first." And because it is grounded in "innate principles" or "natural principles" within man's natural endowment, "the natural conscience subscribes to the equity and goodness of it." [13]

How Willard brings the two poles of divine legislation and human obligation together in natural law requires a larger perspective on God's overall government of his entire creation. The general axiom, of course, is that God governs all things in accordance with their respective natures. To do otherwise would call into question the wisdom of "the great Architect."

> He gave them a nature prompt to their work. He doth not require brick of them and deny straw. He fitted them, by leaving an impression of their natures answerable to the laws of nature, which he laid upon them, to be guided by;

12. CB, pp. 364, 381, 565, 622–25, 649–51, 622*, 656*.
13. LEG, p. 24; EP, p. 187; CB, pp. 143, 567.

so that *the law which was their rule, and their natural con-*
stitution, answered one the other exactly. (Emphasis added.)[14]

This applies across the board with all second beings, but
it falls out into two different ways of governing creatures to
their ends. First, in God's *common* government, creatures
blindly, unknowingly, and passively pursue their appropriate ends. Not so causes by counsel. "Man was made a
reasonable creature, and God would treat him in a rational
way." Therefore, second, in God's *special* government,
where *active* service is rendered to the "God of Nature,"
the creature is obliged to follow voluntarily the natural
law of its own "being and operation." For God to force
man in any way would vitiate the integrity of man's being
as a free moral agent. While man is free to rebel against
the law of his own being, he can never escape from the
natural moral law which forms the fundamental constitution of human life. It is the rule by which God judges,
and speaks directly to man through his own natural conscience.

Man's natural conscience

Because the moral law is internal to man's own being,
something ingredient to human nature as such must witness to its goodness and equity, and this is conscience. To
be human is to feel the presence of conscience, an internal
compass pointing the needle of one's whole life towards
the proper end of human being. This is distinct from the
subjective desire for happiness, because conscience points
towards the objective end, God. Admittedly, some feel it
more than others, and the degree of presence fluctuates
within each human breast during different times and circumstances. At times it appears to be "asleep for the

14. CB, pp. 121, 137, 573.

present," but not for long. Conscience can even err, at least in the short run: "many a man, through the deceitfulness of his heart, and false opinion of himself, passeth a wrong judgment on himself." But what no man can do is "extinguish conscience": "A natural conscience is inseparable from a reasonable creature." [15]

Man's conscience is not "a faculty or power distinct from the understanding," but rather one side or dimension of his rational soul. The human mind not only searches out the theoretical nature of reality; it also "guides him in practice," telling him how best to obtain his proposed goal. Through judgment the practical understanding evaluates and renders a verdict to the will. When the understanding "exerts itself *with respect to the law of God,* and makes a judgment of it, then it is called conscience." (Emphasis added.) [16]

The moral law which conscience subscribes to covers the entirety of human actions, interior thoughts as well as exterior deeds. This means that the witness of conscience cuts immediately into the vital center of personal existence where man is most fully and freely himself, and where God alone by right shares with the self a perfect knowledge of the inner man. One crucial implication of this is that "man's conscience, as such, is liable to no other judgment but that of God." Therefore, no society can legitimately demand one to disclose the content of his conscience or go against it. Social morality and the judicial process through which it operates "can reach no further" than man's "outward behaviour." Only God and the self search the heart.[17]

As a philosopher Willard believes that conscience is natural to "man as man." His argument on this, however, is indirect, for no man can penetrate into another's in-

15. TBM, pp. 139, 140, 149; cf. CB, pp. 508f.
16. CB, pp. 573–74.
17. CB, pp. 575, 580.

terior life. But "every man hath a conscience in him"; this is "witnessed by his own conscience, for he experienceth such a thing." [18] Some ignore it; others repress its voice; but it will never be annihilated. Bought off for awhile, yes; permanently silenced, no. And when man's natural conscience is awakened the life story of the self as it has moved through its historical career will be evaluated according to the natural moral law. Each will know himself as God already knows him.

The law of love

Willard succinctly expresses the basic character of the natural moral law in this one sentence: "God required nothing in his law, but love." The natural moral law instructs man that his well-being rests in loving all realities in direct proportion to their objective, inherent goodness. The greater the goodness of the object, the greater love man ought to have for it. "That which attracts our love to it, is the goodness which we apprehend to be in the object of it, which renders it a thing lovely." And since "it is the loveliness of the object that attracts our love to it," it follows that the lovelier the beloved actually is "the more intensely ought" man's affections "to be let out upon it." [19] Not only does each step in the ascending ladder of being that stretches from the lowest entity to God motivate man to love it according to its proportionate goodness; the law written in man's heart obligates him to order his love into a corresponding hierarchy.

An apparent paradox, however, emerges at this point. Since God is goodness itself, he deserves "all our love." How then can anything other than God be loved without

18. CB, p. 585.
19. LP, p. 9; WG, p. 37; CB, p. 601; TBM, p. 485.

violating the moral law? If love goes to something other than God, does not this mean that some of our love is not centered on God? Obviously Willard rejects such a parcelling out of love which treats God and created beings as though they were "things co-ordinate" on an identical plane or similar field with God playing the role of the greatest one amongst the many. "Now God is goodness itself, whereas other things are only good by participation." Therefore, a radical difference in the way in which they are to be loved appears. One's love for created beings is to be in subordination to one's love for the increated "fountain of being." [20]

> God and our neighbor do not stand upon even ground, so as that these must divide our love and obedience between them; but though it may seem to be a paradox, yet it is a great truth, that God must have all our love, and yet our neighbor must have some of it too. He must have our whole heart and soul, and yet the other must have our hearty and undissembled love. And this would be a contradiction, if it were not for this subordination. But here is a manifest solution of it, viz. God stands as the ultimate object, and highest end and center of all our love, to whom it is to be directed *finally and intentionally*. But the creature in some things stands between us and God, and is to taste of our love as it goeth along to him, though still it is to pass through the creature, and not to rest till it determines in him. As a river that in its course washeth the shore, and refresheth the lands it runs through, but yet goes along and ceaseth not till it falls into the ocean, where it loseth itself. And the reason of this is, because God is the chief good, and last end of all things. Whereas, though other things may bear the relation of an end to some things, that are in subordination to them, yet in order to the last end, they are all but media, and he is the end of them. And hence, what a man doth for the subordinate end nextly, he doth it *virtually and inten-*

20. CB, pp. 584, 139.

tionally for the last end. And hence, let a man love his neighbor never so passionately, yet if it be ultimately for any other respect but for God, and his glory, his love will not be reckoned to him for obedience. (Emphasis added.)[21]

Or as Willard more compactly puts it in his little treatise, *Brotherly Love:*

Our supreme love is due to God, who best deserves it, and it ought ultimately to terminate upon him: but then there is the creature which must also participate in it in subordination to God, and man more peculiarly.[22]

Love is due to both God and created being, "but it neither acts in the same manner, nor is it to be in the same degree." In regard to God the moral law requires "a most superlative and extensive love" by the "whole man." Love to God ought to be singular and total: "It is like a conjugal love, which one alone can share in, and if any go about to divide it, they destroy it."[23] Absolutely nothing else should compromise one's ultimate loyalty and love to the source of all being and goodness, who alone deserves to be loved in and for himself.

But one cannot love God absolutely if one does not also love what God creates. All reality exists through participation in God, and insofar as something is, it is good and exercises a claim upon one's love. This inferior type of love is to be measured out according to one's *self-love.*

Self-love is carefully specified by Willard in such a way that distinguishes between "sinful self-love," where one loves oneself ultimately, and "regular self-love," where one loves oneself proportionately.

This regular self-love, is the rule of our loving our neighbor. As our love ought not to center in our selves, but to extend

21. CB, p. 583.
22. BL, p. 230; cf. LP, p. 4.
23. CB, p. 583.

to others, so in our application of it, we ought to take our measure from our self-love, to regulate us in our love to others.[24]

To fail to love oneself as God intends is to undermine one's affective relationship to the world. Self-haters, Willard emphatically maintains, are disobedient to the laws of nature and nature's God: "there is a love which is due to a man's self, without which he cannot perform the duties of the law which belong to himself." [25]

In loving one's "neighbor" or "all second beings," one's love is to be proportionate to the degree of centrality the created object holds to human being. This means that the hierarchical levels within man's natural endowment set the criteria of value. Living creatures are more valuable than non-living things. Animals are closer to man than plants. Another person occupies a similar station with the self, and while love is due to all creatures, it is due to one's fellows in the family of man in a way that stands far beyond that love for other creatures who rank below man in the great chain of being.

One way of expressing the difference between the manner of loving fellow human beings and other creatures is to start with the negative assertion that neither is to be loved in and for itself as if it were purely and simply an end. God alone is an end in and for himself—all other ends are also means. But lower creatures are a means that can go through man on their way to the final end. A fellow man, however, is a means that points *immediately* to God. Therefore, in loving a fellow human being one's love should not flow through the person, back through the self, then to God. Rather, it should flow exactly like self-love, that is, through the means directly to the chief end, God.

24. CB, p. 584.
25. CB, p. 584.

This entails that man's love for his human neighbors should be "without dissimulation" and should have "the same sincerity" that he has in regard to himself.

> His love to his neighbor must not be outside and comple-
> mental, but inward and cordial. For it is a duty that he firstly
> owes to God, who requires the heart in all, and searcheth the
> hearts of all, and cannot but be displeased if he sees us
> hypocritical in any part of our obedience.[26]

While the love for fellow man is the same in *kind,* Willard argues that it lacks an equality in *degree,* for the love due to friends and family is more intense than that due to "the greatest strangers, and the worst of men."

> That we are to love all equally alike, is in vain asserted by
> some, and flows from the ignorance of the relations which
> God hath fixed among men; unto which he hath annexed
> those special duties, which are to be discharged by a special
> love one to another. There are some to whom we owe only
> a love of benevolence, which commands our beneficence: but
> others deserve our love of complacency.[27]

And the various degrees of our love should be governed by the closeness of relationship between our neighbors and ourselves.

> Every man owes the first and principal of this love to him-
> self. Every man is his own next neighbor. The rule laid down
> [to love your neighbor as yourself] doth not require a parity,
> but only a similitude. I owe charity to others, but it must
> begin at home.[28]

Extending outward, the intensity of love declines, but never does another man, no matter how unlovely his ac-tions, deserve one's hatred. Hatred is the prime alienating

26. CB, p. 585.
27. CB, p. 585.
28. CB, p. 585.

affection, and while there are many wrong ways to be united with one's neighbors, there are no right ways to be alienated from them.

"Shall any be so brutish," Willard asks rhetorically, "as to reject such a law which is so suited to the natural inclination of the reasonable creature?" [29] Irrational as it may seem, men in fact do go against the law of their own being. And when they do a chasm opens between man's own teleology and the natural moral law, emptiness invades the heart, an affective alienation erupts, and human bondage results. Rebellion against God's will for his own creation commences with a misjudgment of the goodness of being which triggers off a civil war within man's breast that ever enlarges to enslave the whole man through internal conflict. Spiritual paralysis is the plight of the rebel.

29. CB, p. 585.

CHAPTER SEVEN

The Rebel

*Man in his creation was like a fair house, new built,
fit to entertain the King of Glory, fit for a temple for
the Holy Ghost to dwell in; but now he is like an old
house gone to decay, where, by the ruinous heap, we
may guess what a famous structure it once was, but is
now nothing but rubbish. . . . He is held in passive
subjection to the law, though he doth not actually
conform unto it. He is not properly an outlaw, or
put out of the reach of it, but a rebel.*[1]

Anomy

The opening move in Willard's analysis of the "rebel"
within each human heart begins with the nature of sin,
which he cryptically identifies as "anomy, or a transgression
of the law, by a cause by counsel, or a moral agent." [2] Were
it the case that man lacked spirit he would never have been
exposed to the possibility of rebellion.

It is certain that sin can be charged upon no other creatures,
but such as are causes by counsel. A beast cannot be said to
sin, and why? but because it hath no moral powers in it;

1. CB, p. 157.
2. BRGK, p. 45.

it cannot make a rational and deliberate choice, but is acted
by instinct.[3]

Where brute animals act "blindly," men share with the
angels "a power of reflection upon themselves," that is,
human consciousness exercises the power of doubling back
upon itself so that the self is both subject and object.[4]
Willard never commits himself on when children develop
this decisive self-reflective power. Prior to that time, though,
they "cannot sin *actually*." (Emphasis added.) Until children make "use of their rational powers" they are only
potentially spirit and strictly speaking are not yet capable
of a *human* act.[5]

On emerging as a free moral agent man witnesses within
himself a "swerving of the rational nature from its rule." [6]
Reeling from the shock of recognition, man discovers that
he is "losing himself." The presence of anomy or lawless-
ness within a moral agent can be detected in any one of
three distinct ways that a human act may deviate from the
law of love certified by man's own natural conscience.

First, "the matter of the action" may violate the letter
of the law.

> The rule prescribes the things themselves which are to be
> done, the action is required of us; not to do this, or to do
> something else besides it, is the most gross and apparent
> sinning of all; and this is that only which men can directly
> and immediately charge upon others, ordinarily.[7]

The public world is limited to concrete behavior that
breaks the law explicitly, for only the outward manifesta-

3. CB, p. 214; cf. p. 184.
4. CB, p. 181.
5. CB, pp. 197–198; cf. TBM, pp. 262, 291.
6. CB, p. 209.
7. CB, p. 189.

tion of a human act is open to the inspection and judgment of other human beings. God and the self, however,
suffer under no such limitation. They probe the vitals
from a much more profound vantage point, and they know
that "a man may fail in his duty, and be guilty before
God of sinning against him, in the very action wherein
he keeps most close to the letter of the law, and others
cannot charge transgression upon him." The reason for
this difference arises directly from the fact that God and
the self share inside access to both the "manner" and the
"end" of an act. So, second, even when the "matter" of
an act is well within the law's specifications, if it is performed without cheerfulness, or in slavish fear, or with
reluctancy, then the "manner" of that act is spoiled. And,
third, an action is defective if the "end" exhibited in
the act "centers short of God as the last end." [8]

If any given human act swerves from the law in any
one of these three ways, then that act is morally deficient,
and the agent of that act stands in guilt before God, regardless of whether or not any third party hears about it.

The sinfulness of a rational and spontaneous human act,
it should be obvious, "doth not arise from the nature of
the action, as it is an action, but from the moral deficiency
of the agent." Succinctly put, "no action, *qua action*, is
sin; sin being the anomy that cleaves to it." Viewed from
a metaphysical perspective "every act hath an *entity* in it;
and is so far good." This means that even a sinful act involves "the exerting of a natural power, by applying it to
an object; and so there is a natural goodness cleaving to it
as an act; nor can it be done without divine co-operation."
The evil of a sinful action, rather, lies with its "obliquity,"
when viewed from a moral perspective. Moral judgment

8. CB, pp. 189–90; cf. WG, pp. 36–37.

concerns the "respect that it bears to a rule, by which the agent is obliged, and either agrees with it, or is repugnant to it, and so is either right or wrong; and this repugnance denominates it sinful." Therefore, even though God sustains a sinful act, this "doth not in the least make God the efficient cause of the sin," because sinfulness is "accidental to the action." The guilt of a sinful act "terminates on the man himself." The agent alone is morally deficient; his action is infected with "anomy," not because he expends his natural energy, but because he freely acts contrary to the law of his own being.[9]

Because these abstract distinctions operate in the analysis of every concrete action, a single example will suffice to exhibit their thrust. In their sexual expressions brute animals can never deviate from the law precisely because they lack self-reflection and are driven by instinct. Moral considerations simply do not arise. Even though from a physiological perspective human beings do not function sexually in any critically different way from brute animals, moral considerations are paramount and deviations are notorious. In terms of the "matter" of an act, every illicit sexual act is sinful. But even licit acts may be warped. For example, a husband may exploit his wife by using her as merely an extension of his self-centered lust. Although the "matter" of his act might be perfectly acceptable within civic morality, before God the "manner" and the "end" of the act are defective. Nevertheless, *as act* even an adulterous act is still good. To claim that a sexual act *qua act* is evil is to deny the goodness of God's creating and sustaining activity. But to deny that a human sexual act may be contaminated with anomy is to remove it from the sphere of *human* activity.

9. BRGK, pp. 19, 24, 38; CB, pp. 179, 203, 213.

After granting that the overwhelming majority of men are committed to overlooking the magnitude of their rebellion, and are eager to avoid personal responsibility for their own betrayal of the law of love, Willard still is of the persuasion that at least in their more lucid moments "all men readily confess that the condition of mankind is troublesome and sorrowful." Had Willard met someone who seriously denied the actuality of this condition, he would have responded to the denial with an incredulous smile and dismissed it as the workings of a mind so naively lacking in self-awareness as to stand below the need of rebuttal. The Puritans had tasted damnation in their own mouths and felt "an hell in their own breasts," and so far as Willard could tell any honest man with the slightest acquaintance with himself, not even to mention his neighbors, would acknowledge as a fundamental given in the human equation the potent presence of "anomy" eating away at "the delight" of life. And "life is truly life no further than it is delectable." Even high-minded pagans who failed to penetrate conceptually to the profounder levels of malaise within the human condition had at least glimpsed the consequences of man's despair-producing situation: "Plato complains that the soul hath broken her wings, and such like." And "heathen moralists" using only the light of nature quite obviously had addressed "actual sin." By carrying the analysis far beyond the single deviate act into the ground or principle from which it arises, however, Willard reaches beyond the realm of civic morality into the interiority of man's private terrain. The truth about man is that "the frame of his heart" is fixed on a teleology that runs "contrary to the law of God." The project man imaginatively entertains to give meaning and value to his life over a spread of time cuts straight across the proper end of human being; therefore, every conceivable participative act in that project is necessarily infected with the lie. A "crooked bias" warps the vital center of "the natural man." [10]

The natural man

Probably no words Willard systematically uses lend themselves more readily to misunderstanding than "nature," "natural," and "naturally," for they can point in radically divergent directions. In the first instance "nature" denotes that which is essential for something to be what it is. In the case of man, "human nature" in this first sense refers to man as a reasonable creature. Regardless of the particularities of one individual's life-story or the religious state he is in, he shares with all men an essential nature, and this nature is good. But in the second instance, "nature" denotes man in revolt against God and estranged from the law of his own being. "Nature" in this second sense signifies the corruption of "nature" in the first. "The natural man" is a grotesque distortion of what man was created to become. This second thrust is exhibited in all the following bald assertions. (Emphasis added below.)

The heart of every *natural man* is estranged from God.

There is a practical atheism in the heart of all *natural men*.

Man is *naturally* a stranger to the power of godliness. . . . The *state of nature* since the apostasy, is a state of alienation from God. [11]

In some sentences both meanings are present. For example, when Willard claims that "the *natural* man cannot by his *natural* power move one step towards God," this means that "the natural man as one alienated from God cannot

10. MM, p. 247; TBM, p. 190; CB, pp. 209–11, 225, 444–46.
11. MM, pp. 46, 54, 287; TBM, p. 190; PT, p. 35.

move one step towards God by exercising any power within his inseparable natural endowment as a reasonable creature."

The concern in this section on "the natural man" is with those whose life-relationship to God is one of "enmity." [12] The exact referent of this "natural man" is every human being in the religious state of apostasy. To labor the obvious, Willard viewed himself as being "a natural man" prior to his experience of God's gracious forgiveness. According to his analysis of the human condition, no man escapes anomy when he emerges as a free moral agent with the power to deliberate with himself and choose for himself an end. On discovering that he has to answer for his life man immediately moves to secure his own well-being within himself, and this necessarily pits him against God's kingdom. He is in league with the Devil and his hosts.

Willard believes there are a multitude of real demons, but he ordinarily refers to them as if they were one being, the Devil, or Satan, or "the god of this world."

> The Scripture often speaks of them, in the singular as one, partly because they are united in their great and general design; their kingdom is not divided, but there is an unanimous agreement whereby they consent as one person against God and man: partly because they are subjected to one Prince, to whom they yield a diabolical obedience.[13]

This spirit of negativity was not created by God. It arises rather from an angelic revolt in the courts of heaven. Willard repeats the mythological account of how the apostate angels in pride rejected God's positive appointment of angels to minister to the needs of the lower ranking earthling, man. In their spiteful rebellion they set out to blas-

12. CB, p. 210.
13. CB, p. 180.

pheme God and murder the souls of men. While God does not divide his sovereignty with this spirit of negativity, he does permit Satan to assault the divine-human community with "equivocations, untruths and falsehoods." The devil can only seduce, he can never love. The deceiver can only detract, he can never enrich the world. The counterfeiter can only tempt, he can never compel his targets to comply:

> he not only would not force [man's free will] by violence, for that the human will is not capable of, but he could not morally alter or change it, or put any new principles into it, for he was a creature.[14]

But from such an exposed position Satan exercises power through "man's consent." The only real power "the god of this world" holds over the human commonwealth is that delegated to him by man, but men are transparently eager to bow down in obeisance to the dark powers: there is "always a party in us ready to betray us into his hands." [15]

Deep within the convolutions of man's consciousness lurks "a spy watching its season and advantage." This "spy" in us is "a principle of concupiscence, which is unto temptation, as tinder or gun powder is to fire, on which if a spark do but fall, it takes." So potent and uncanny is its power that even "if there were no Devil in the world, there is enough in our native concupiscence, to sow the seed of a temptation in us, to ripen it for the birth, and to bring it forth." [16]

In the full context of Willard's thought Satan's function is primarily that of making vivid the crucial claim that man will serve some master, that man must live as a citizen within some kingdom that captures his loyalties and loves:

14. CB, p. 182.
15. CB, p. 183.
16. MM, pp. 209, 182–83; CE, pp. 58, 83; HG, p. 6.

Man was not made for sovereignty, but for service, and properly for the service of God. If therefore he shakes off this service God righteously provides him cruel and tyrannical lords, that shall bear rule over him.[17]

"Self-sovereignty" is a capital illusion, and decked out in the disguise of "self-sovereignty," Satan moves from triumph to triumph.

In the short run natural men are overjoyed by the fact that they can "walk in the way of their hearts, and the sight of their eyes." On the face of it, the rebel "tasteth a great deal of sweetness in his beloved sin." His feelings of delight, however, soon begin to suffer corrosion under the impact of the discovery that "the world's cup may intoxicate you, but it can never slake your thirst." True, it does relieve the "earthly part" of man, but not the rational soul that yearns for felicity in and through completion: "while it feeds the body the soul starves: It is not itself soul-food." When measured against the yearnings of the human heart for an infinite good, the world is a wasteland, not because there is anything wrong with the world, but because the sensualist has inverted the order of creation. He thinks that his life is to be found in that which ranks below him in the great chain of being: what he was ordained to be the master of is the master of him. Not only is the visible world incapable of satisfying his insatiable appetite; as creature comforts slip away from him he senses that "the inchoated miseries of this life" mark out his future, for "there is something of death in every misery." Increasingly invaded by a "sense of misery and emptiness," he clutches at counterfeits to fill the enlarging vacuum.[18]

The self-server's journey into the wasteland, moreover,

17. MM, p. 109.
18. CB, pp. 6–8, 177, 209, 223; MM, pp. 46, 68, 89; FO, p. 19; TBM, p. 134; SM, p. 12; WPTC, p. 163.

is not straightforward, for he has to share the world with other actual agents also in the process of becoming. Although he will find plenty of encouragement from many of his fellows, especially when they profit from his folly, he quickly learns that the society in which he lives will enforce some restraints upon his behavior, the "matter" of his actions. Undoubtedly he will protest "any curb or check" upon his self-aggrandizing moves, but even if he should subvert the given social order a new one would immediately assert its authority. Such is the providence of God. If he is a dedicated sensualist, he will have to adopt the disguise of a moral man and with cunning deceive his neighbors. As an openly avowed policy self-centeredness is worthless in any conceivable human society.

After a few turns with the powers that be and much instruction from those primarily responsible for the preservation of the social order, the natural man may glimpse the advantages of bringing his behavior into line with the minimal limits necessary for a common life. After all, "No man in his right mind can be so fond of sorrow, as not to be willing to have some lenitives applied to it, for the easing of the grief of it." And one of the palliatives readily available is to conform: "there is a rational conviction on conscience, which on the awakening of the moral principles in men, maketh them to look upon these and those sins to be brutish, and puts them upon rejecting them, and taking up of contrary courses." [19]

Little repentances of this sort are clearly possible until death, at least in principle:

> There are few sinners, if any in this world, that are so utterly debauched, but that they have some principles of morality abiding and active in them; which are a civic ornament to them, and so far commend them to the liking of men.

19. DJ, p. 143; MC, p. 2; SM, p. 70.

There is an active principle in him, which may be wrought
upon and excited, so as to receive the habits of human sciences, and common morality.[20]

Not only can men through their own resources avoid further violations of the letter of the law; better yet, "there is
a great deal which a man may do in morality, by the improvement of his natural powers . . . which belong to the
nature of man." These powers are part of his natural endowment and endure "as belonging essentially to humanity." Willard even goes so far as to argue that

. . . the very heathen moralists, who only followed the light
of nature, could boast that they found incomparably more of
pleasure and satisfaction, in the exercise of their virtues, than
the greatest sensualists could possibly do in their fleshly
pleasures, and could reject these with scorn for those.[21]

But it still remains the case that "when he abstains from
the things that the generality immerse themselves in, and
lives contrary to the current of the times . . . the moralist
doth not put a force upon his whole nature, though he may
suppress some exorbitant motions of it . . . but he grati-
fies his moral principles, when he curbs in these which are
sensual." [22] Strenuous suppression admittedly is better than
running with the pack, yet it can never center man's heart
on his proper end, and therefore is never sufficient to overcome the "split" within man between his actual project
and the proper end of human being.

The moralist, of course, does not realize this. By scaling
down the reach of the moral law to cover only external acts
in the public domain, men "think it an easy matter to pay
all observance to it; and when men are thus persuaded, they
can live very well satisfied in themselves." The rub comes,

20. CB, pp. 239, 434.
21. MRL, pp. 8, 11.
22. MRL, p. 11; cf. SM, p. 60; MC, p. 41.

however, when the mind becomes sensitive to the fact that moralistic contractions of the ethical community violate man's essential being. God is not such an absent-hearted lover as to be satisfied with mere external observance of the letter of the law of one's own particular body politic. Even though man "can indeed do the material part of duties," so long as this is not performed "after a right manner, from a right principle, or for a right end," it is "nothing but a few narcotics, to stupefy, and not in the least to cure that malady." Cognizant of the truth that "it mends no man's condition, to be opprest by a law," Willard casts a solemn warning into the teeth of the moralists who advocate suppression as a way to wholeness: "Take heed then of skinning over the sore of natural corruption, by outward restraints; if your soul be not healed, you will die of it." [23]

Once he has cut through the conventional pieties and discovered that "outward restraints" will not carry him into "the harbor of felicity," the rebel may try religion. Aiming all the time at serving themselves, the natural men of legalistic stripe "make fair pretences, and are huge sticklers for God and his ways." These hypocrites may fool the world and the church, and even themselves for awhile, but never God. He knows that "the most religious natural men have chosen the service of God, not as their end, but only as a medium to attain some other end by." [24]

Self-abandonment, moralistic suppression, religious formalism—the life-styles of the natural man are multiform, but throughout them all appears the decisive pattern of living from and for himself. Following a trajectory that arises from basic mistrust and aims at self-sovereignty, the natural man "hath in him a rooted prejudice against God."

23. DJ, p. 143; CB, pp. 210–12, 225, 228, 569; MC, p. 2.
24. CB, p. 177; MM, pp. 42f.

The longer this malignity festers within, the deeper his affective alienation from the world and himself grows until it becomes a chasm and he is haunted by a sense of emptiness. But no matter how drugged he may become, the rebel against God's kingdom cannot finally obliterate

> . . . the conviction which every natural man carries upon his mind of his absolute dependence upon God, and that he alone can make him happy or miserable: for, although this be a truth which man by his sinful courses practically contradicts, and a light which he is not unwilling to extinguish, it is yet so riveted in the mind of man, that he cannot wholly evade it; it flicks as close to him as his being.[25]

Even when he is locked in "a deep lethargy of carnal security," the natural man senses that he is championing a lost cause. And as he begins to realize that he must face God and answer for his historical career he is afflicted by an uneasy conscience.

An uneasy conscience

The anchor point in Willard's understanding of man's response to his guilt is that "everything is to the mind of man, as he resents it [that is, as he feels or experiences it]. If the man be ignorant of the evil, he is not troubled by it." [26] In deliberating with himself, every man evaluates his own actions in the light of some norm.

The reason the sensualist experiences "sweetness" in his acts lies in the fact that he does not acknowledge the rightful claims of any law beyond himself; therefore he evaluates his actions in the light of his own hedonistic vision of the good life. When society blocks his reckless pursuit, or

25. MM, p. 15.
26. TBM, p. 134; see *Oxford Dictionary of the English Language* s.v. "resent."

punishes him if he is caught in the act, he is filled with hostility against the social authority that frustrates his spontaneous good fun. Along this path he comes to regard society as evil.

The reason the moralist feels so self-satisfied lies in the fact that he has risen above such low-grade self-awareness and judges himself in the light of the norms he has internalized from his provincial society. In his own eyes the moralist who has successfully made the transition from an adolescent to an adult frame of mind is in an excellent position to celebrate his own virtue and to castigate his neighbors for their beastly behavior.

In the presence of God, however, "those that are best disposed morally" are in worse shape than "the most ill disposed, and rough hewn," because they are much more inclined to justify themselves when the Spirit of God presses home the claims of the ethical community that embraces all creaturely reality and God. On viewing himself in the light of the law of this community, man's natural conscience begins to strip away all the masks behind which man hides from himself, and to shatter all the mirrors in which he fondly nurses idealized reflections of himself. When his conscience becomes sensitized man inwardly begins to realize the magnitude of his betrayal of life and love. Now he experiences "a sinking and overbearing perplexity of mind."

In one of his fuller treatments of the natural conscience, Willard carries the discussion through six distinct offices.

First, conscience is "a statute book" in which is indelibly inscribed the natural moral law. Second, it is "a register" infallibly recording "all matters of fact" that a man does in his lifetime; though he forgets something now, it is still very much there and will be read by him "sooner or later." Third, it is "a witness" that is "privy to all" human actions, even "the most secret sins"; and it "dares not withold

its testimony, when God commands it to declare." Fourth,
it is "an accuser" which "will haunt them with its reflections, and give them no rest." "And though, for the present, men bribe and baffle their consciences, and make them
to hold their peace, yet they will certainly betray them. . . .
Yea, how often doth it blab all, and force a confession from
them before men." Fifth, it is "a judge" which "keeps a
court in the man" and "calls the man to its bar." And
sixth, conscience exercises the office of "an executioner"
when it "falls upon the man, and rends and tears him."
"It begins to feed upon him here in this world, it fills
him with horror, and many times precipitates him into
mischief." [27]

> It is guilt apprehended that torments them, and makes them
> feel a hell in their own breasts; they start and fly at the
> shaking of a leaf, and would run away from themselves, if
> possibly they could.[28]

When panic grips the heart of the rebel as he vainly tries
to run from himself, he gets a clearer picture of what he is
up against: "Guilt is a prison that holds the man fast: the
bars of it are too strong for the whole creation to be able
to break." [29]

At first blush it is not obvious that guilt enslaves man,
for absolutely nothing ever takes away "the natural freedom of his will." Regardless of what monstrosity any given
man may have committed, it does not subtract from the
spontaneity of the present elective acts of his will. Even the
most habituated criminal still has "a spontaneity in his
elections, and his will is not forced." [30]

27. CB, p. 259; TBM, pp. 131–40; cf. CB, pp. 229–30, 447–48.
28. CB, p. 208.
29. TBM, p. 135.
30. CB, p. 211; BRGK, pp. 14–15.

But guilt corrupts this natural freedom in such a way that man continuously justifies himself and repeatedly defies God's law of love, and each new act of opposition to God's government of the world "contracts a new guilt" to fire the antagonism.[31]

> It is not this or that sin in itself, that holds the sinner bound under the curse; for, let it have been what it will, or what sort of degree soever, yet if men do truly repent of it, that will turn away the wrath of God, and take off the threatening from them: but it is impenitency added to it, that continues a man under the curse, and perseverance in it, that makes his case to be remediless.[32]

Repetition rivets the rebellion so deeply into man's self-justifying posture that he is morally incapable of re-orienting "the frame of his heart" towards his proper end, even if he wanted to. Freely he chooses to reject that life with an open future. Freely he refuses to embrace the good that is laid out before him. Try as he might, "he is extremely cross to a closure with the law of God." What this means affectively is that he is progressively filled with hatred against the present real possibilities of being. As long as he remains in this hostile condition man is utterly impotent to liberate himself from his guilty past. Run from it for awhile, yes; escape from its icy grip, no. He can no more free himself from guilt than he can free himself from his past. He must live with the whole story of his career through time.[33]

He who was created for communion with God lies in bondage, a prisoner within the kingdom of sin and death. One of the heaviest chains crushing the human spirit in this

31. CB, p. 203.
32. BFD, p. 285.
33. CB, p. 210.

satanic empire is guilt: "one way in which sin hath dominion is by guilt." Another one is the dread of death.

> As man cannot find his life in himself, so neither shall he mend himself in the world; he goes but from one want to another, from a famine within doors to a famine abroad. If he goes to the world he dies, and if he rests in himself he dies. He doth but rise to fall, he doth but go abroad to meet with that death which was coming home to him.[34]

As it sinks thoroughly into his consciousness that "man begins to die as soon as he begins to live, and he goes on till he is swallowed up of death," the flames of joy flicker out. Feeling cheated out of his rightful inheritance within the created world, every relationship within it becomes embittered: "they can taste no more relish in any thing here, than in the white of an egg." Joylessly the rebel goes on living after a fashion, but his life-force has been blunted. "The life of life is the delight which we have in it, and if that be separated, it is but a living death." In this dreadful condition the satanic illusionist, who initially coaxed him to "count sin to be nothing" and opened endless ways to reduce his sensitivity to guilt by avoiding self-examination, plays out the last card in his hand: "he then would make our sin appear great beyond the extent of a pardon, so to precipitate us into despair." Succumbing to this hopeless state, man becomes "an intolerable burden to himself." [35]

What began in basic mistrust and proceeded through alienation terminates in despair, "the clearest emblem of hell upon earth that can be." Although a civil war rages within the rebel's breast, he is "a stranger" to the way of peace.[36]

---

34. MM, p. 88.
35. CB, pp. 8, 206, 228, 446–48; RAD, p. 68.
36. MM, p. 180; HM, p. 11; cf. WG, p. 35; CB, pp. 324–25.

Man's present condition

To leave people endlessly "poring upon their own misery" in abject despair is the last thing Willard intends by his reading of man's present condition. Repeatedly he points towards the way of peace secured in God's gracious forgiveness of rebels, for no manner of amount of betrayal forecloses on "the sweet invitations of the Gospel." [37] Surrounding his analysis of the human predicament is the triumphant conviction that

> There have been such as have added to their natural folly, prodigious wickednesses, whereby they have expressed the height of their madness, who yet notwithstanding have been made partakers in this grace to be heaven's favorites, and taken near unto God, and entitled to all the glories of his kingdom.[38]

That this is not merely a dialectical point with Willard is powerfully registered by the existential situation in which it was preached. The quotation is drawn from a sermon in which Willard was making a last effort to reach one Sarah Threeneedles shortly before she was executed in 1698. Willard states that Sarah "belonged to my flock, and had received the seal of the covenant from my hands, and was under my charge." But Sarah was one of the local whores in Boston who had been "the unhappy mother of two illegitimate children successively, and become the barbarous murderer of the latter of them; for which crime, she there stood under sentence of death, upon due conviction, and that before she had seen full nineteen years in the world." On top of that, while imprisoned awaiting execution "she renewed the crimes of her unchastity; she gave herself up

37. MM, pp. 195, 180.
38. IS, p. 10.

to the filthy debauches of a villain, that was her fellow-prisoner." [39] An impenitent sinner, she.

After carrying Sarah from reflecting on "what an egregious fool" she had been, to the shortness of time she had left in which to make her peace with God, Willard solemnly advises her in the presence of the congregation that

> There have as great sinners as you, sought mercy, and found it. God can be just, and yet forgive your sin; he can get himself a name, and exalt the glory of his grace, in you; he can make those falls of yours to be the occasions of his appearing in his grace the more eminently to you, in his humbling, healing, and pardoning of you; and so making it to appear in you, how much more that can do for the saving of a soul, than a vile hardened sinner can do for his own undoing. Only beware of cheating yourself by any fond presumptions of mercy, though you live in your impenitence, or of supposing that you can comply with the terms of peace in your own strength.[40]

Regardless of how profoundly a soul has been disrupted, God's grace is sufficient to heal and pardon. The healing process, however, comes only as a gift from above; never does it derive from some source within man.

How Willard understands the healing process will be considered in detail below. Here the negative implication needs to be stated as unequivocally as possible, namely, that left with only his natural endowment man completely lacks the possibility for engaging in communion with God. The chief end ordained for man transcends the grasp of man's natural powers. This being the case, is not God then at fault for creating a being who cannot possibly reach fulfillment through his own strength, no matter how hard and seri-

39. IS, "To the Reader"; cf. Cotton Mather, *Magnalia Christi Americana*, Book 6, vol. 2; p. 364.
40. IS, pp. 22f., 27–28.

ously he tries? Has not the wisdom of God misfired by
creating something in vain? Willard argues to the contrary by insisting that this humanly impossible situation is
the just punishment visited upon the children of men because of Adam's act of treason in the Garden of Eden.

> When we look all over the world, and see sons and daughters
> of sorrow scattered up and down upon the face of the earth,
> born to affliction as the sparks fly upwards; when we see sick-
> nesses, diseases, deaths, perplexities, disappointments, dis-
> contents, and all manner of miseries, let us stand still and
> inquire, how a creature so excellent in his creation, is become
> so sorrowful and miserable in his present condition; and to
> satisfy our minds about it, let us look back to man's apostasy,
> and there we shall read the text on which all this infelicity is
> the woeful commentary.[41]

From the actualities of man's present condition experienced
in varying degree by all human agents, Willard proceeds to
justify the ways of God with man through a speculative
account of the creation and fall of Adam. The predominant
intent of his effort is to remove from present agents any
excuse for their situations and to show that fullness of being
can flow only from a new fountain opened within God's
own life.

41. CB, p. 158.

CHAPTER EIGHT

The Creation and Fall of Adam

When God had made man he placed him near to himself, having put his own image upon him, endowing him with such grace as fitted him for communion with his maker; and to bind him forever to love and obey him, he plighted a precious covenant with him, engaging his love and favor perpetually to him in case of his being faithful to his duty; but threatening him with his infinite displeasure in case of his disobedience. Matters thus standing, man, by the instigation of Satan was allured and invited, and by the abuse of his own free will led away to fall from his obedience, and become a covenant-breaker; whereby a wall of separation was set up between him and God; and the peace thus broken, war was proclaimed between God and man.[1]

Who is Adam?

While it is indisputable that Willard believed that roughly six thousand years ago there lived an individual person named "Adam," he presses on immediately to the larger truth that "Adam" refers to every human person: "But when God created man, he made only one man, and

1. CB, pp. 307–08.

one woman, and called their name *Adam*, which is a common name for the whole species." "Adam" is present in us, and we are in him, for he is "a public person, representing the whole cluster of mankind."

> Before we had our actual existence, we were virtually in his loins; as the effect is virtually in the cause. The rose is virtually in the bush, before it so much as buds. . . . And when we actually be, we are actually in him.[2]

Since he is the "common head" of the "common stock," every man has his "inbeing in Adam." Adam is not only the proper name of a singular historical figure; his is the common name for the family of man.

The union wherein those who come after us as well as those who have come before are all bound up together in "Adam" is derived from the sexual ties that link one generation to the next: "It is by natural generation that we have our inbeing in Adam." Although an individual's rational, immortal soul, which is the locus of human agency, is not generated through the sexual act, man is essentially embodied, and through the body man lives in a human world that is organic.[3]

From the actuality of this organic union Willard established Adam's authority to act in behalf of his progeny.

> . . . we are in him, as in the root, the common principle of all his posterity. We are so united to him, as to be considered as having our inbeing in him in all respects.
>
> For,
>
> (1.) He had a paternal right to this. Gen. 1.28. God said unto them be fruitful and multiply. Hence we are all said, to have one father. He was the first father of men; and hence we were under him, as children are under their parents, and

---

2. CB, p. 195.
3. See above, chap. 5.

involved with him as they are. And we know that a paternal
right is of very great influence. Run up all the generations
that have been, and they will end here.

(2.) He hath a regal or princely right. For, being the father,
he was also the prince of the world: and here kingly authority first took its original. Now all subjects are involved in
their prince as so, and he transacts their public affairs for
them. Adam therefore bore the image of all his children upon
him.

(3.) He was the root of all mankind, and they are the
branches. Now it is natural and rational that the same sap
which is in the root, should spread itself. So that this union
of ours unto Adam, hath respect to all the relations and
changes of state, that he, as our root, was liable to. We were
to be, as he should be in all those respects.

(4.) Adam stood not as a private, but a public person. Not
for himself, but for us all; he was the representative of, and
received the common stock which belonged unto mankind.
All the estates of all that were to be born of him, were put
into his hand, and he was to trade for them. There was at
first no other man besides him, and all were to descend from
him, he therefore had their whole concern betrusted with
him, as their common head.[4]

To be human is to live in a family that Adam heads by
"natural right."

Every man's "inbeing" in Adam, it should be pointed
out, relates only to his "public" self, for only in that sense
does he represent mankind. Otherwise he is a "private person," and citizens of the realm, so to speak, are involved
in and concerned with the prince's "public acts" only, for
in these alone is the shape of the human story exhibited.
This means that each of us is, first, a participant in Adam's
sealing of a solemn covenant with God which embraces
both God and man in an overarching constitutional struc-

4. CB, p. 196.

ture. And each of us is, second, a participant in Adam's act of disobedience against this government, his betrayal of his pledged love. Only these two acts by Adam are public and therefore representative of mankind.[5]

What would be the systematic implication if the union between every man and Adam were denied? Willard's argument from this counterfactual supposition is straightforward:

> If there had been another generation of men in the world, that had derived from another original, they would not have been involved in this affair [i.e., the covenant of works], nor come under this fall. Adam would have had nothing to do to transact for them.[6]

Released from representation in Adam's public acts, what then would the human situation look like? Man would still be, and know himself to be, a creature, a being by participation. Furthermore, from his nature as a cause by counsel, man would still know that he was also a spirit, a creature capable of deliberation and choice, and responsible to God for his actions. Not only would man realize he was passively a subject of God's common government which rules over all the visible ranges of being, some of which are as close to him as his own flesh. He would also know that as a reasonable creature he was subject to God's special government where active service is due, for the moral law by which God governs has an internal witness in man's natural conscience. In a word, he would still be a moral agent under the moral law as a rule of life. What would be lacking would simply be his having the moral law "as a covenant" with both "a promise made unto obedience" and "a threatening to disobedience." "The law as a rule saith, this thou shalt do, and this thou shalt not do. And

5. CB, pp. 195–97, 200, 285, 367; cf. TBM, p. 93.
6. CB, p. 199.

as a covenant it saith, if thou do so, thou shalt live, if otherwise thou shalt die." [7] Without the union with Adam the present individual would be in a situation similar to that of the angels who lack a covenant with God: some obeyed, others disobeyed. The moral law abides, but each one would answer for himself alone.

On two accounts this counterfactual discussion is instructive. First, it shows that Adam's public acts—his sealing and falling from the covenant of works—are informed by the biblical record, but that man's moral agency and voluntary character stand on quite a different footing, one that is secured by right reason working with the light of nature. Second, if and when an individual is engrafted into Christ he is liberated only from Adam's public acts. Adoption into Christ frees him only from the law as a covenant, not from the law as a rule. As a rule, the moral law is permanently written into the fundamental constitution of human nature as such and is obligatory upon all men regardless of whether they remain "in Adam" or come to be new men "in Christ." But irrespective of what destiny any individual may have, every man has a stake in Adam's public acts, for each person begins his life in a human world already committed to God's covenant with Adam and already contaminated by man's treason.

The essential nature of a covenant

Prior to addressing the particular covenant Adam sealed with God in the Garden of Eden, it is imperative that the essential nature of every covenant be clarified. The concern here is with the nature of any given covenant regardless of whether it is the covenant of works or grace, the old or new covenant, the covenant of reconciliation or redemption,

7. CB, pp. 151, 567; cf. LEG, p. 24; EP, p. 188.

the national or church covenant, a marriage or business covenant.

Willard programmatically describes a covenant as "a mutual engagement between two parties." In unpacking this general description he specifies three features that are necessarily involved in the nature of a covenant.

First, a convenantal relationship properly obtains only between "two parties." Even though numerous persons may be involved in a particular covenant, from a constitutional point of view there can be only a party of the first part and a party of the second part. For example, "all the subjects in a kingdom" are one party and "their prince" the second party.

The second necessary ingredient is that the "obligation" contracted must be "voluntary."

> The word covenant, used in our text, implies a mutual obligation, and voluntary, between parties, comes from a root which signifies to choose, because in a covenant there is a choice of parties and conditions.[8]

Negatively expressed, this second ingredient excludes all but causes by counsel from participating in covenants. Without the power of choice there would be neither the possibility of nor need for a promise:

> . . . natural necessity destroys the very nature of a covenant. For, a covenant is a voluntary obligation between persons about things wherein they enjoy a freedom of will, and have a power to choose or refuse. It is a deliberate thing wherein there is a counsel and a consent between rational and free agents.[9]

For man to be a promise-maker and a covenant-keeper it is absolutely fundamental for his self-commitments to be

8. CK, pp. 3, 5f.; CB, p. 331.
9. CR, p. 68.

voluntary. Strip away this freedom and covenants become impossible.

A personal transaction involving a voluntary obligation between two parties, however, still does not make a particular engagement a convenantal relationship. Were these two ingredients alone sufficient, a covenant would not be essentially different from "bills, bonds, mortgages, or whatsoever of the like nature." The decisive factor that sets a covenant apart from those types of transactions is the third necessary ingredient, namely, that the obligation be "mutual." The mutuality of the interchange is crucial, for the obligation and security embrace both parties. Each party is equally committed to and bound by the "terms" of a covenant.

The "terms" of a covenant specify the "conditions" which must be met in order for the promised consequences to take effect, and also the threatened penalties for any failure to comply with the conditions agreed upon. The *formal* structure of every covenant must be hypothetical: if x, then y; if non-x, then non-y. Negatively this entails that if and when a promise is made without a conditional clause, then such an "absolute" promise fails to constitute a covenant, though it is still binding upon the promiser.

In order to appreciate what Willard has riding on the distinction between an absolute promise and a convenantal promise, notice how he speculatively argues this theological point. God *"might* therefore, had it seemed good in his eyes, have acted merely as a sovereign, and promised life and salvation, *illimitedly* to these or those according to pleasure; but because he hath *chosen* to deal with man in the way of a covenant, therefore he doth not so do. An absolute promise cannot be a covenant-promise, because it contradicts the nature, and takes away that which is essential to a covenant." God could have refused to engage man in a covenantal relation, but it in fact did not please him to exercise his right as Creator and act out of "mere lordship, or sovereignty." Rather, he chose to relate to man through the rational means of a covenant. God freely took upon himself constitutional limits and is bound by the terms just as surely as man. Prior to sealing the agreement each party is "at liberty, or stands free," but after once entering, a party is "not now at his pleasure whether he will do or not do." Each party voluntarily submits to the other. Each is vulnerable to loss through the other's betrayal of personal trust. Both pledge their solemn word of promise to abide by the conditional terms.

Even though conditions are constitutive to covenants, two radically divergent types of conditions should be carefully differentiated.

First, "antecedent conditions" are those in which there is a commensurability between the condition and the consequence. Because the condition is met, the agent merits, earns, and deserves the fulfillment of the promised consequence. Covenants with antecedent conditions are of a "legal" tenor, really a quid pro quo.

Second, another type of covenant operates with a "connex condition" which simply occasions the promised consequence. Lacking commensurability, fulfillment of the condition in no way merits, earns, or deserves the fulfillment of the promised consequence. A connex condition is simply "the way and means of conveyance, *by* and *in* which God gives the things which are promised, but not *for* which, and yet without which they are not given." (Emphasis added.) Willard even notes in passing that "it is a frequent Hellenism to put [if] for [when]." (Brackets in text.)[10]

Perhaps a few commonplace examples would help to point up the difference expressed in these subtle distinctions, diagrammed in this distribution.

10. CK, pp. 5–12; CP, p. 91; cf. CB, pp. 153, 276, 310; DJ, p. 436; UI, p. 10; BFD, p. 28; MC, p. 90.

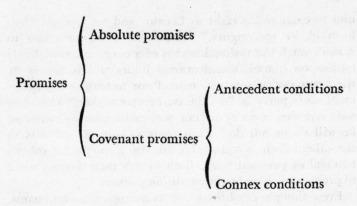

If a father promises his son $100 next spring, then he is personally obligated to give it even if the son disappoints him in some unexpected way. Since no terms are specified this promise is "absolute" and therefore is not covenantal at all.

But if the father promises his son $100 next spring in return for the son's labor during the winter, then if the son fails to perform the work prescribed he holds no claim upon the wage, but if he does carry out the terms the father is morally obligated to pay. This is a covenant with an "antecedent condition."

But if the father promises his son his entire estate when the son returns from England after being graduated from Cambridge, then if the son returns with degree in hand the father is obligated to fulfill his promise, although the son's return itself does not in anyway merit the gift at all. This is a covenant with a "connex condition."

The type of condition within a covenant determines whether its tenor is "legal" or "evangelical," and the substantive difference between a "legal" antecedent condition and an "evangelical" connex condition is precisely the formal difference between the covenant of works and the covenant of grace.

The covenant of works

Adam's initial public act is the sealing of the covenant of works with God. (Frequently this covenant is also referred to as the "old" or "first covenant"; in the Westminster Shorter Catechism it is called "the covenant of life.") "And man was no sooner made, and placed in his station among the creatures, but God enters into bonds with him, and takes him into covenant." Why should God do this? And why should man accept? To secure man's obligation to serve God by obeying the moral law? By no means, for man "owed service to God as he was his creature." Had Adam rejected the terms he would not have ceased being a cause by counsel, a moral agent under a rule, anymore than he would have ceased being God's creature. So he must have had a reason for accepting the terms of the proffered covenant. The motive is God's promise to reward perfect obedience with blessedness, a never ending life of uninterrupted joy, the complete fruition of communion with his Maker. A corollary threat follows hard on the heels of the promise: disobedience to the law deserves a rupture in the communion, and this spells death. Through the covenant of works man's situation is expanded from that of being simply a reasonable creature to that of also being a consenting citizen who acknowledges God's rightful authority within a constitutional framework. Adam voluntarily consents to the terms.

In agreeing to the stated terms Adam pledges himself to running the race of God's commandments to perfection. "Man stood now a probationer for happiness or misery; the covenant told him how he might escape the one, and gain the other: by offering the reward to encourage him, by threatening the penalty to caution him." [11] By creation

11. CB, p. 153.

man was neither happy nor miserable—he was only *capable* of being either, a capability he shared with the angels, and a capability not open to anything less than a reasonable creature with the power of self-reflection. Happiness is not something man has a *natural right* to expect. Only through the covenant does he acquire this *conditional right*.

Why did God submit to the covenant of works? God was under no natural necessity to enter the covenant. He could have treated man differently. He did not have to hold out an exterior reward to coax man into doing his duty. God could have let things ride with man as he did with the angels. (In this type of speculation one option is not open: God could not treat man immorally or unfairly, for to do so would mean that God would violate his own essential being which is the very foundation of justice.) But God voluntarily "restrains himself" and in fact engages in a covenant which obligates God to man. God grants man a claim upon God's goodness. No reason is sufficient to account for this gift. It is as unfathomable as God's creative love for expressing himself in and through a world other than himself. That God opens the possibility of eternal happiness through the covenant of works is simply God's way of relating to man.

> Those glorious rewards of obedience could not become his [man's] due in any other way [than through a covenant]. He owed service to God as he was his creature, but God owed him nothing, but what he should please freely to give him. Obedience was but his duty, and there could have been no merit in it, nor could he have challenged a reward of life for it, if it had not been covenanted for on this condition; for God is voluntarily and not naturally obliged to any of his creatures.[12]

12. CB, p. 153.

Two free parties, neither of which is under any compulsion whatsoever, mutually pledge to each other a solemn oath to respect the inviolable terms of the covenant of works. Even though they are "unequals" in terms of power, both are equally bound to the specified terms of the covenant. God and man are now locked in a common bond which absolutely nothing can abrogate—God is truth itself, and to go back on his word is inconceivable.[13]

The character of the covenant of works is "legal" for it functions with an antecedent condition which requires "entire and perfect conformity to the will of God." Although the antecedent condition and the consequent reward are not exactly proportional to repay services rendered, they are commensurable and the fulfillment of the condition deserves, earns, and merits the reward. "Man in the first covenant had to do with God immediately." To be precise, in the covenant of works man is concerned with "God out of Christ." [14]

In claiming that the covenant of works has a "legal" tenor, Willard does not deny all manner of graciousness. To the contrary, when grace is "taken in a larger sense" to mean that which is given freely, then of course "there were abundance of grace" in the original contract. Not only did God freely bring into actual existence from the realm of pure possibility a world that lacked an intrinsic necessity for being. Not only did God bestow upon man the gift of freedom and moral agency with the possibility of communion with God, a possibility no other creature in the visible world ever dreamed of entertaining. Beyond these, God even voluntarily engaged this singular creature in a covenant which obligated both parties within a con-

13. Cf. CB, pp. 153, 217, 285, 339, 354, 378; CR, pp. 78f.
14. MRL, pp. 17f; CK, pp. 4, 18; TBM, p. 542.

stitutional framework. While all this sprang from God's gracious benevolence for man, it was surpassed in beauty by the critically important gift to Adam of "the image of God." [15]

The image of God

Because of the centrality of "the image of God" within Willard's system, its exact denotation should be carefully considered. His systematic usage of "the image of God" excludes two meanings that had wide currency in traditional theology, and unless this is clearly understood his body of divinity will be decisively misinterpreted. In one clarifying passage he states his position unequivocally:

> I know there are divers sentiments of divines, about the image of God, which was on man at first; some there be who distinguish between the natural image, and the moral; making the former to consist in the rational powers, of understanding and will; and they divide the latter into external, consisting in his dominion over the creatures, and internal, consisting in the habits of grace or holiness put into him: but I reckon this last, or the internal moral image, to be the only thing that is designed in Scripture.[16]

Willard's pivotal reason for limiting "the image of God" to "the habits of grace or holiness" arises from his belief that "the image of God" is "not essential to his humanity, but separate from it." Regardless of his religious state, however, man retains both his "rational powers" and "his dominion over the creatures" because these are part of his essential being and position. Throughout this study, "the image of God," in accordance with Willard's intention and usage, refers exclusively to "the habits of grace

15. CK, p. 15; cf. CB, pp. 271, 377.
16. CB, p. 210.

or holiness." This divine image, in fact, is a supernatural capability given to Adam in addition to his natural endowment. It consists in the superadded gifts of "those graces of sanctification, by which man was fitted for universal perfect obedience to the whole will of God." [17]

Why does Adam stand in need of a supernatural gift over and above his native resources? Because God created man for communion with himself, and this communion requires perfect holiness, that is, the fullest possible measure of wholeness of which a reasonable creature is capable. This supernatural capability definitely does not enable finite man to become infinite in power: "It must be the measure of a created, and not an increated perfection: God is infinite, man is finite, and all his perfections limited." The superadded gift does not dialectically denigrate man's natural power; rather it endows human nature with the real possibility for realizing itself to the highest pitch of expressive power it can possibly bear. The absolute call to fullness within the human spirit is what moves God to imprint his image on Adam.

> . . . for to require that of a creature which it was never in a capacity of complying withal, had been unworthy of God's infinite wisdom, and altogether inconsistent with that justice which God laid the foundation for, in the nature and state that he created man in.[18]

God is "no Egyptian task-master, requiring bricks where no straw is given." Adam was equipped with the power to obey perfectly the conditional requirements of the covenant of works and thereby merit felicity. Notice that blessedness is deserved within the constitutional framework; God only grants Adam the ability to keep the condition.

17. CB, pp. 125–26, 210–11, 263, 377; TBM, p. 190; CK, p. 15; cf. EP, p. 169.
18. CB, pp. 125–26; FO, p. 73; cf. MM, pp. 71, 80; LEG, p. 25.

It [the image of God] was then a stamp and character of divine goodness left upon the nature of man, making him able to perform the service that was required of him. And it was not implanted by the rule of nature, but by the rule of divinity; neither was it from the principle of nature, for then it was inseparable. Hence it may in some sense be called *natural,* in other *supernatural: natural,* as it is due to the nature of man made for such an end, without which he could never have attained it; and *supernatural,* being a more glorious excellency than the bare principles of nature can exert.[19]

Attention should be focused on the fact that Willard believes that "all the faculties and powers both of soul and body, received the stamp" of the divine image. It is "not this or that part of him"; it is not an isolable facet in Adam that stands alongside other dimensions of human being. Rather, as the demand for completion extends to the whole man, so likewise Adam's "whole nature" was imprinted with the image of God and empowered to act in perfect obedience. What this means specifically in terms of man's cognitive powers is that the understanding of the reasonable soul was sanctified, that is, Adam could discern the truth and regulate his life accordingly without going through the experiment of trial and error. And his volitional power was "enabled," "inclined," and "disposed . . . to choose the good, and refuse the evil, by a free, full and perfect elicit act." Furthermore,

In the affections and outward man, it [the image of God] was that which inclined him to an entire subjection to the commands of the sanctified understanding and will, without the least reluctancy, or being prest to obey them; so that he was in a readiness for every good work. The body as well as the soul, the sensible as well as the rational powers were fit for

19. CB, p. 125.

their business, and there was no pravity or disorder in this whole frame; but he was every way fitted, both to will, and to do, needs no other evidence, than that less than so, could not have fitted him for his end, or denominate him good, in the station he was put into, under the special government of God.[20]

"Now these sanctified powers in him, could not but approve, choose, and love the law." [21] Not only was Adam's natural endowment superlative—his moral rectitude was splendid. As Adam came forth from the hand of his Maker, he was outfitted to perfection. He could have reached his ordained end, he could have obeyed perfectly the law of his own being, he could have deserved the fruition of communion with God because he could have fulfilled the antecedent condition of the covenant of works. Communion with the infinite God was a real possibility open to finite Adam. Had this original possibility not been genuinely open, then tragedy would have been built into man's very nature as man. Had Adam not been in a position to meet the demands his own nature placed upon him, his cosmic outcastness would have been morally justified. He would have held an ultimate metaphysical warrant for filing a complaint against God because he would have been saddled with an essence that defied completion. But man's essential being is good, he could have reached his ordained end, because Adam had "the image of God" stamped upon his entire natural endowment to orient him properly towards the service of God. Why then did the "probationer" fail so miserably during the initial confrontation with the dark powers? To understand why God and Adam suffered a "falling out," it is necessary to examine Willard's interpretation of the sacramental seals

20. CB, pp. 126; cf. pp. 209, 263, 284, 560.
21. CB, pp. 566; cf. 311, 377.

which God positively appointed to ratify the covenant of works.

The sacramental seals of the covenant of works

God appointed two "sacraments" to seal in a visible way the mutual agreement on the moral government of the cosmos. Willard is well aware of the fact that the term "sacrament" is not "used expressly in the Word of God," but he quickly adds that the church had appropriated it "to express something which is pointed to in the Word of God." And Willard even notices that the term is used rather loosely in the writings of the patristic age: "mystery" is translated as "sacrament." Yet from the earliest generations Christian thinkers had also "put a more narrow sense upon the word," and it is this more confined meaning that solicits Willard's interest here.[22]

As a word "sacrament" is derived from the ancient Roman "military oath that was given to their soldiers when they were listed in the army." In this oath the soldiers bound themselves to be "true and faithful to their service and subjection," and this oath was accompanied by a rite to seal the agreement. Willard puts strong emphasis on the visibility of the rite. A sign must stand "objectively before our bodily senses" in order to qualify for sacramental action. As a sensible sign, a sacrament has two dimensions: the visible sign itself and the spiritual object it signifies. The form of union between these two sides flows solely from divine appointment. Negatively put, it does not proceed from any natural correspondence between them (as a cloud signifies rain). Neither is it a conventional correlation (as a red light signifies stop). The union is anchored exclusively in God's *positive* ordination: "God

22. CB, pp. 834–38.

being pleased to make use of sensible things, for the further-ance of spiritual good to the children of men, hath ap-pointed these things to be used, by us for that end, and hath therefore sanctified them, and put his blessing upon them." [23]

In regard to the covenant of works God set aside two trees to function sacramentally and to reinforce visibly the stated terms. First, in order to "ratify this promise [of happiness] and make it the more obliging, he sequestered this tree [of life], and put that figure upon it, that it should be a sign and a seal of the promise, and by looking upon it, he might stimulate himself, and fortify against all temptations to draw him away." Second, corresponding to the threat of death in case of disobedience stands the tree of knowledge.

> It was to let him see and know that God was in earnest; and would be as good as his word; that the threatening was not merely to frighten him, but to ratify to him the truth of what he was warned of. This tree also had a further design in it, viz. to be a special trial of his obedience. This tree, as the former, had nothing in its own nature, to make it un-lawful for man to use the fruit as common food; but God to show his sovereignty, did by a positive law, lay a restraint upon man's liberty, and so exempted it, to see if he would acknowledge his sovereign, and give him his prerogative. Not that all obedience was restrained to this one article; for the whole moral law was his rule; but here was a special proba-tion of him; so that this tree was both a sacrament, and a test unto man at the first.[24]

The substantive core of the covenant of works is the *natural* moral law, but it is precisely the *positive* cere-monial law God appointed to seal the covenant that oc-

23. CB, p. 841.
24. CB, pp. 155; cf. pp. 15, 191–92.

casioned Adam's fall from innocence into moral confusion
and spiritual death.

Adam's fall from integrity

Adam's genuinely open possibility for achieving his
ordained end of communion with God also leaves open
the counter-possibility of failure. Ontologically considered,
this means that even with "the image of God" Adam's
essential being still remained mutable. "Absolute immutability," according to Willard, "is a prerogative of God,
and belongs to him alone." "All created perfections, though
never so eminent in themselves, yet have this defect attend-
ing of them, that in themselves they may be lost. Adam
was one thing, and his rule another; as they might meet,
so they might part. And this mutability in the moral agent
is a ground of the possibility of its falling, and so forfeiting
all its perfections." [25] For a cleavage between Adam's
actual life and the law of his own being to occur at all
there must be this mutability. In calling mutability a "defect," however, Willard is not in any way compromising
the goodness of created being; rather he is specifying one
decisive difference between created and increated being.

Besides the ontological possibility of fallenness present
within man's mutable nature, Adam was concretely tempted to actualize this dark possibility and divorce himself
from "his rule." God allowed Satan to assault Adam
through lies. Because Satan lacked direct access to man's
mind prior to the corruption of his "fancy or imagination,"
Satan "entered into the serpent" so that the temptation
would proceed through the outward senses of the body.
Therefore, while the serpent is a passive instrument in

25. CB, p. 186.

the temptation, "the serpent itself was not at all to be blamed. Blame is only merited by a fault that is committed; and every fault is a voluntary transgression of a moral law, prohibiting it, and such a law can be given to none but causes by counsel; and hence, no unreasonable creature can be blameworthy by any of its actions." Blame for the temptation falls rather on the Devil, for he is the active agent. As "a thief, who collogues a traveller out of his way, upon pretence of showing him a nearer and better [way], and so draws him into some blind corner where he robs him," Satan always operates "under the pretence of truth and goodness . . . to seduce man to believe a lie and thereupon to entertain evil." [26]

He proposeth a short and easy way to be happy at once, by eating the fruit of this tree. He therefore abuseth the name of it, to insinuate a secret virtue hidden in it, to fill man with divine wisdom, and advance him to a God-like perfection. And he knew if he could but screw into man an opinion of being happy by it, he could go a great way to prevail upon him.

He calumniates God, as having some ill design in prohibiting man the use of this tree. q.d. God knows how much a very taste of this fruit will advance your perfection, and because he envies you so much felicity, therefore he hath forbidden you to touch it, lest you should thereby be made more happy than he is willing to have you.

He persuades them that the threatening was but a bugbear to fright children, and not to be regarded; and gives his word that there was no damage in it, so to remove them from all fear of any misery likely to ensue upon their undertaking to eat of it.

Hereupon he offers the fruit to them in its loveliness.[27]

26. CB, pp. 180–84.
27. CB, p. 183.

While Satan is the prime instrumental cause of Adam's fall and is therefore blameworthy, it still remains the case that Adam "had a power of resistance" against all the wiles of the Devil:

> The tempter could only tempt. He could not compel. All his strength lay in his subtlety. Man's free will is incapable of compulsion. It was therefore in its own nature a thing contingent, whether the temptation should prevail or no. The Devil had no physical power over man's free will, he had only the cunning of persuasion, by presenting his covered fallacies.[28]

But "by a deliberate and consulted act" from the vital center of his inmost being, Adam "embraced the temptation, and so threw himself into the transgression." Adam was "the principal cause" of his own undoing.[29]

Eating the forbidden fruit of the tree of knowledge, of course, was not sinful simply because of anything *naturally* ascertainable in the "apple" itself. Indeed, from the perspective of the light of nature alone, Adam would have been in the wrong had he *not* eaten it.

> In the order of creation, God made these things for the use of man, and he gave him the dominion over them. Man's bodily life was to be sustained by things fitted for that end; and this fruit was so suited, it had no noxious quality in it, but had that nourishment, and pleasancy in it, that was adapted to man's appetite, and wholesome for him. . . . The act of eating is natural, and so lawful, yea necessary, and the fruit was convenient to the end of eating.

> By this common law, I mean the law of nature, which was engraven on the heart of man, consisting of all those rules, which directed him to righteousness and holiness; and were suited to his nature, and imprinted on his conscience. This

28. CB, p. 185.
29. CB, pp. 186–87.

[law] told him that he was to make the glory of God his last end in all things; and to improve all the creatures that were put under him according to their natures and usefulness, for the advancement of this glory by them. Now according to that light, man had reason to think, that he might glorify God, by a thankful eating of that fruit as well as any other; nor could he have conscientiously abstained from it without superstition.[30]

Not the *natural* moral law but the *positive* ceremonial law alone was broken, and this infinitely potentiates the offense. Adam's sin was not a slight nibbling around the edges of legality, an adolescent testing of the limits. Adam deliberately attacked the core of his relationship to God; he contemptuously opposed the very symbol of God's "lordship," he subversively set his heart on supplanting God's actual governance of the world. "He did, therefore, by this act, as it were, tear off the seal from the covenant, that was past between God and him." [31] The ontological and moral integrity of all being, symbolically represented in the seals of the covenant of works, was violently rejected by Adam.

Adam's revolt, it should be emphasized, was not just a single deviate act, but "a complication of many actual sins." The act of eating was only the terminal stage of the rebellion. The initial act began in the vital center of the reasonable soul.[32]

. . . there was a faith or trust in God required of man in his integrity, by virtue of the first command; which faith was to have been placed upon God according to all that he revealed of himself to man in the first covenant; and was to be the spring of his obedience. He was to believe him to be such a one as he manifested himself to be in all his declared per-

30. CB, p. 191.
31. CB, p. 192.
32. CB, p. 214.

fections; to believe the truth of his commands, or his promises
and threatenings. And it was a wound in this faith at which
the apostasy began, which if our first parents had preserved
in its vigor, they had never yielded to the temptation.[33]

Once losing faith in God, Adam "entertained the arguments of the enemy, believed them, and was thereupon
dissatisfied at the command, and so more eager in his
desire to be tampering with it." Vulnerable to suggestion,
Adam jealously imitated God and tried to ground his life
in himself, but "standing alone by himself," Adam "lost
himself." [34] Pride, not sensuality, forms the core of the
fall of Adam:

> God had set him as high as a creature could well be; he stood
> next to God, subordinated to no other order. All visible
> creatures were put under him, and the angels themselves,
> though in divers respects more noble beings, yet were made
> to minister for him. There was none above him but God;
> nor any being equal to him, but the holy angels; and yet he
> aspired to be climbing higher, accounting his own place too
> low for him.[35]

The prime locus of Adam's first transgression lies not in
the bodily appetites; rather, the "rational powers were
chiefly concerned in sin." But from this corruption within
Adam's ungrateful and unfaithful heart the poison spreads
out to contaminate the "whole man."

> All the faculties of his soul, and powers of his body were
> interested in it actually. His understanding had assented to
> it, his will had given its consent, and made the choice and
> resolved upon it; his affections carried him forth, and spurred
> him on to it; his ear had received the false reports; his eye

33. TBM, p. 539.
34. CB, pp. 192, 311.
35. CB, p. 193.

had been deluded by the fair show; his feet had carried him to it; his hand had taken it, and his mouth had tasted it.[36]

As the whole man rejected God's command, so the whole man suffers the disorder that follows. The threatened consequence of "death" permeates the entire human enterprise.

In Adam's fall we sinned all

As all mankind is represented in Adam's public act of sealing the covenant of works, so all mankind is represented in Adam's public act of betrayal. Admittedly, it was his own "personal act":

> Adam was the prime and personal offender; the action in which the transgression was, was his own, he was the subject of it. God then laid it to his particular charge, as the person that was immediately interested and concerned in it. Every action as such, terminates in the subject, and so did this.[37]

Nevertheless, Adam's "personal act" of disobedience was also a "public" act, and therefore it is "imputed" to all his posterity "because their persons were legally in him, as the person of the debtor is in the surety, as the person of the prince is in the ambassador." Consequently, "the whole cluster of mankind" represented in Adam suffers the penalties this public transgression merits: "His act of treason hath tainted all of his blood and posterity deriving from him." [38]

As a direct consequence of the fall of Adam, the open friendship and loving freedom that characterized the original relationship between God and man degenerated

36. CB, p. 192.
37. CB, p. 196.
38. CB, pp. 196–97.

instantly into a relationship expressed in images of raging conflict: "the peace thus broken, war was proclaimed between God and man." [39]

What this warfare entails for Adam's posterity is that each human being is deprived of "the image of God." All the superadded gifts of grace that sanctified Adam's entire nature are now lost without a trace. The divine image is "wholly defaced, and there are not so much as any relics of it left." [40] It should be emphasized, however, that in losing "the image of God," Adam did *not* forfeit his derived authority over the visible world or his reasonable soul. That which is essential to human nature as such endures through any and all religious states. But man's natural endowment does suffer disorder because of Adam's fall. His whole life-force *deprived* of the image of God for its orientation, "the image of sin" rushes into the vacuum, and the essential being of man becomes *depraved*.[41] "The image of sin" extends over the whole man, perverting him in ways diametrically opposed to "the image of God." Just as "the image of God" was not another part of Adam, so neither is "the image of sin" another part of "the natural man." It is, rather, an infection of the entire natural endowment, beginning with the understanding and proceeding throughout the complete essential being of every man.

> Those corrupt principles do fill the whole man. They are not only in him, but they run through him, and wholly occupy him; he is a mere lump of opposition to God and his ways.
>
> For,

39. CB, pp. 307–08.
40. MM, p. 288; CB, p. 210.
41. TBM, pp. 190f; CB, p. 560; MRL, p. 8.

This corruption hath wholly perverted his superior faculties. Man is principally and most properly accounted a moral agent, by reason of his understanding and will: for it is by virtue of these that he is to be treated after a rational manner; and therefore the most woeful efficacy of this deprivation is to be seen in these.

In his understanding. This was to be eyes to him, to point out his way; and not only is it become blind and ignorant in spirituals, but perverse too; it is filled full of cursed principles, which pervert and lead it out of the way; he calls good evil, and evil good; he judgeth of things just contrary to the truth; he reckons the service of God to be unprofitable, and the service of sin only advantageous and delectable: accounts man's felicity to consist, not in the fruition of God, but, in some other thing: and this judgment rules him. Hence this corruption is to be seen.

In his will. This was to govern his elections; but not only can he not choose God for his portion, but he is wilfully set, and inclined to stand, at an everlasting distance from him.

It hath violated his inferior faculties and powers; making them servants to sin. What this influence is, is not easy to describe; but we know that all are the subjects of sanctification. 1 *Thes.* 5.23. and therefore they are under this pollution.

Hence,

In the affections there is a crooked bias. These are the feet of the soul, the handmaids of the will: but these are become exorbitant, all of them falsely placed, and violently acted, in a wrong way, and on wrong objects; he not only doth not love God, but he hates him, *Rom.* 1.30. not only doth he not hate sin, but he loves it, and insatiably desires it.

In his senses and members, he is enslaved to sin. . . . Every thing in him, his outward senses, his eye, his ear, his taste, his hands, his feet; his inward senses, his fancy, cogitation, memory, all are ready to execute the commands of his depraved will, and yield obedience to every lust of concupiscence; so that there is nothing left in him but that which is unclean.[42]

As the whole man's "disposition," "natural bent and inclination," "bias," or "frame of the heart" was oriented towards God in the religious state of integrity, so in apostasy the core of every man's being is now turned away from its proper end and actively seeks fruition where it cannot possibly be found. As long as this "frame" defines a man's life and shapes his actions, he is "necessitated to sin," though this necessity does not in the least infringe upon the voluntary character of his actual sins.[43]

How this pollution is communicated from Adam to all his descendents Willard is at a loss to explain. In regard to "the physical way or manner of its derivation," he admits candidly enough that

> I must needs confess mine own ignorance about it, nor am I able to give a natural reason for the derivation of this pollution, or how it is propagated, or what is the influence by which the formative [animal and vital] spirits are polluted, or how they can communicate this sinfulness to the reasonable soul. And all the arguings that I have met with on this subject, seem obscure and unintelligible. And I believe it is one of the judgments of God which are unsearchable. It is then a point of faith.[44]

The plain facts of the matter, however, demonstrate, to Willard at least, that "the contagion cleaves close to human nature."

A circumcised Jew begat an uncircumcised son. The best of men have sometimes the vilest children. And there are none

42. CB, p. 211.
43. CB, pp. 198, 209f.
44. CB, p. 198.

but are sinful. The natural birth cannot be such as will prevent the necessity of the new birth.[45]

All men are born into a family contaminated by Adam's
fall. And from the polluted fountain within our own
hearts actual sins flow ineluctably to increase the misery
of the human community. God would be justified in al-
lowing the whole tribe of rebels to sink into the abyss of
alienation. No man holds any claim upon the favor of
God, for Adam forfeited "life" when he broke the conditional terms of the covenant of works and brought down
upon his posterity the threatened consequence of "death."

Permissive providence

Although man is the principal "blameable" cause of his
own undoing, and so is responsible for the transition within
the divine-human community from integrity to apostasy,
from love to hatred, from joy to despair, from communion
to alienation, from peace to war, from life to death, it still
remains the case that God is actively involved in the transition too. Power does not flow from the human side alone.
While "God and man were once friends," God made it
possible for a "falling out" to transpire. Indeed, God caused
it to happen, yet he did it in a "blameless" way.

Willard specifically addresses three "blameless causes" of
the apostasy of the human race. First, the divine law itself
was the occasional cause of human disobedience: had there
not been a law, there could not have been any violation.
Second, the eternal decrees of God's absolute foreordina-
tion are exempted from blame, for the eternal decrees are
immanent in the secret life of God, not transitive acts af-
fecting the world. Although nothing whatever will ever
"come to pass against or besides God's will," God's knowl-

45. CB, p. 198.

edge of the future does not place "any compulsion" on man's
freedom to act. "Freedom of causes by counsel is no whit
infringed by it, but ratified; because in it, God hath pur-
posed that free agents shall act freely." Furthermore, "Man
could not do it [i.e., sin] in compliance with the decree,
because he did not know it [i.e., the decree]; and if he had
known it, it was not his rule." [46] The revealed will or the
law, not the secret will, is the rule by which man is to
live and evaluate himself. But, third, it is the case that
God permitted Adam to fall. According to Willard's account, "the greatest difficulty" conceptually arises not with
the immanent decrees locked forever within the secret life
of God, but with "God's permissive providence" that affects
the world.

Willard does not take the easy way out by denying
God's hand in the fall of Adam. "God could have prevented man's fall, as he did that of the innumerable company of angels: he could have kept off the tempter, or have
fortified man's free will with assisting influences, and
determined it, without any compulsion, to have rejected
the insinuation of Satan. . . . No doubt, had God seen
meet, he could have kept up his trading with man in the
covenant of works, confirmed man in his obedience, and
so have made him happy forever in that way." [47] But God
did not so choose. He in fact allowed Satan to tempt Adam,
he in fact suspended the "influences of confirming and
assisting grace" at the critical juncture, and he in fact
sustained the very act of treason itself.

> Not only did he [God] suspend his assistance but he also
> influenced the act itself; else it had never been; all action is
> entirely from the superior cause; Adam could never have
> looked on the fruit; nor deliberated about it, nor consented

46. CB, pp. 178, 103, 106, 134; CR, p. 13.
47. CB, p. 377.

to eat it, nor stirred his hand to take it, nor opened his mouth to taste it, if there had not been an active concourse of the divine power enabling him in the very act, thus to exert all these powers of his.[48]

Still, God is not to blame, for God did not withhold from Adam anything that was owed him: "had Adam asked help of God, and it had been denied him, he might have had something to plead." But Adam refused to ask anyway: "he chose to be without that help, and deliberately consented to commit that sin which was his ruin." In this way Willard argues that even though God is "the supreme orderer" of Adam's fall, "and that according to his permissive will," it still is the case that God "is not in any respect to be accounted the author of sin." [49]

Why did God permit sin to rupture the rapport within the divine-human community? Hideous though sin is, "God was resolved to make sin a foil, on which he would draw the colors of his holiness, in the displays of his justice and grace." Had man never rebelled against God's government of the world, there would not have been "an opportunity for God's showing himself merciful and gracious." [50] Even with the actuality of alienation and its dreadful consequences, the world is richer in value because of Adam's fall, not because of any intrinsic goodness in sin, but solely because more profound depths in the divine life are manifested in overcoming the train of evil consequences flowing from man's love of illusions.

48. CB, p. 179.
49. CB, pp. 179, 186; FO, p. 73; cf. BRGK, entire.
50. CR, p. 81; FO, p. 76; cf. DJ, p. 58; CB, pp. 268–69, 309.

CHAPTER NINE

The Covenant of Grace

The unparalleled and incomprehensible love of God to sinful man, displayed in the wonderful affair of his redemption and salvation, is the great thing celebrated in the Scriptures; and is that which invites our most frequent, and raised meditations. . . . The contemplation of this is truly surprising: time is too short; eternity but long enough to spend in the survey of it. This love is a fountain which sprang up in, and runs down to eternity. It never knew a beginning, nor shall ever come to an end.[1]

The source of the covenant of grace

Even though "the light of nature" casts a searching beam upon the creative and moral moments in the divine life, it completely fails even to flicker in regard to the third moment, the curative, restorative power of God's compassion. Knowledge of this countervailing power flowing from God's "transcendent good will" lies beyond "all the wisdom and understanding of angels and men, which they had in them by nature."

. . . the light of nature can not discover the least tracks or prints of . . . a restitution provided by God for fallen man.

1. CR, pp. 1–2.

. . . the works of creation and common providence had not any Gospel written on them.

Nature's light afforded not a key to unlock this mystery.[2]

The key that opens the mystery of God's gracious movement to restore communion within the divine-human community is God's Word of promise contained in the biblical witness: "this is a matter of mere revelation."

> We are therefore here led by the hand, from the sorrowful and heart-breaking consideration of man's inexpressible infelicity by his apostasy, to the pleasant and soul-refreshing contemplation of his anastasy, or restitution. . . . And truly, the main drift or design of the whole book of God, in the Old and New Testament, is to give us an account of this affair.[3]

The Bible alone discloses God's promise to heal man's brokenness and to provide for man's restitution.[4]

In asserting that God's Word transcends "nature's light" and the grasp of man's natural powers, Willard does not mean that it is something foreign, alienated from the human world, mechanically imposed on man from above. When God calls the human world back into the community of faith, hope, and love, God respects the ontological integrity of man's being. Because God's covenanting Word is "a moral medium" addressed personally to man as a reasonable creature from within the full human condition, the Word can never "work after the manner of a charm." "God accepts of no service but what is done with a willing mind," and this entails a refusal on God's part ever to force a response: "Now there is no obedience but what is voluntary. If the heart and will be not in it, but it be a forced thing,

2. CB, pp. 246f; FO, p. 23.
3. CB, p. 246.
4. See above, chap. 2, fourth section.

it cannot truly be called obedience." [5] God's Word solicits a free and personal response to embrace the terms of "the covenant of grace," which is the constitutional order of the "mediatorial kingdom."

(Willard frequently substitutes "the new covenant" for "the covenant of grace"; less frequently it is referred to as "the gospel covenant," "the covenant of peace," "the remedial covenant," and "the covenant of reconciliation." All of these are different names for the same thing. It should be noted, however, that "the covenant of redemption" is a different, though related, matter, for this is an intertrinitarian compact between God the Father and God the Son; sometimes this intertrinitarian compact is called "the covenant of suretyship." "The covenant of grace," on the other hand, is a covenant made between God and man.)

The most fundamental point in Willard's understanding of the covenant of grace is that "God's grace is absolutely independent of any qualification in the creature." "That the sovereignty of divine grace, which can neither be prevented nor obliged by any thing in or for us, is a pillar-truth of the Christian religion." [6] This triumphant assertion stands at the apex of an ascending series of pivotal beliefs. Mark the parallel structure.

(1) Although God could have remained alone without the loss of any essential value, God in fact freely chose to create a world other than himself to reflect his glory.

(2) Although God could have created a world without any reasonable creatures, God in fact freely chose to create free moral agents who were causes in their own right.

(3) Although God could have related to man without any limitation upon his own divine prerogative, God in fact freely chose to be man's covenant partner by entering into

5. CB, pp. 810–21; 382.
6. CR, p. 121; CB, pp. 250ff, 271ff; CK, p. 76.

a covenant of works which mutually obligated both parties to each other.

(4) Although God could have established man in the covenant of works in such a way that man would never have broken the conditional terms, God in fact freely chose to permit his creature to exercise his freedom in such a way as to betray his pledged love.

(5) Although God could have justifiably left the entire race of rebels rotting in a richly deserved exile, God in fact freely chose to initiate a new covenant to liberate man from the situation his love for illusions had brought into history.

Each of these five steps expresses God's liberality. While God could have acted otherwise, he "arbitrarily" chose to so commit himself. God's choices are perfectly free, for at no point does God stand under the compulsion of some natural necessity to perform any one of these world-transforming acts. No deductive dialectic could possibly squeeze any of them out of the divine essence. That they happened rests solely within God's sovereign freedom. Nevertheless, it is the case that they did occur. The world exists, man is endowed with spirit, the moral order is in motion, and there is a cleavage in man's heart between his own project and the law of his own being. Those are factual claims, open to inspection by any man regardless of his own religious state. And the good news that God acted to overcome the alienation in man's disordered love and to heal man's vital center so that he can joyously consent to being, is also a factual claim, not a deduction. It differs from the previous steps, however, in that it cannot be derived from "nature" by "right reason." Awareness of God's healing power proceeds from God's own self-disclosure contained in the biblical witness, and this revelation can be received in faith alone.[7]

7. CB, p. 293; CR, pp. 67f.

The time of the covenant of grace

According to Willard's reading of the biblical record, the new covenant entered history not with Jesus, Moses, or Abraham, but rather immediately after Adam fell from innocence into moral complexity and spiritual death. The message of God's restorative love "began generally to be published and made known in the world, as soon as man had by his fall brought ruin and misery upon himself." Never has there been a time since the initial rupture within the divine-human community when God's "special grace" was not available to cure man's diseased condition, for God's "mediatorial kingdom" has been in operation "ever since the covenant of grace was revealed to fallen Adam." [8] Willard even goes so far as to claim that "religion hath been the same in all the essentials of it, ever since the fall, and hath received no alteration but in positives. The Gospel was preached to our first parents presently upon their apostasy." [9] For all intents and purposes essential Christianity is as old as the creation of man, minus one day.

The rhythms of continuity in the ways of God with man are so potent in Willard's consciousness that he systematically rejects any equation of the old covenant with the Old Testament and the new covenant with the New Testament, though linguistically "covenant" and "testament" are equivalent. Because God's forgiving initiative is from everlasting to everlasting, Willard argues that

> . . . it is a grand mistake for any to account nothing gospel, but the New-Testament. Indeed, the greatest part of the Old-Testament is gospel, containing the gracious transactions of God with fallen man. Now whenever such a thing is made

8. MM, pp. 306–07; cf. CB, p. 349.
9. MW, p. 11; cf. RGD, pp. 1–7; FO, p. 118.

mention of, it must come under the tenor of the new covenant.[10]

As the church of the Old Testament, Israel proclaimed the same essential message, administered the same covenant of grace and worshipped the same covenanting God. Nevertheless, while the essentials cannot be altered, the new covenant does undergo some positive, ceremonial changes with the rise of "the evangelical dispensation of the kingdom of Christ." Before the time of Jesus the relationship between God and man within the covenant of grace was more external, less spiritual, more concerned with the terrors of the law, less concerned with the comforting promises. In a word, the former regime was "suited to the childish, the latter to the virile age of the church." [11] With the advent of Jesus Christ the same covenant of grace received new means, new sacramental seals, and a new extension. No longer is it limited to the national life of Israel. Now the new covenant is extended throughout the world. The institutional form of the people of God in this new epoch is "the gospel church." [12]

The community of the covenant of grace

In Willard's ecclesiology "the gospel church" is distinguished from both "the church invisible" (the elect within the universal church, past, present, and future) and particular, local congregations of Christians. Without denying that sometimes the term "church" bears both of these meanings in some New Testament passages, Willard argues from 1 Corinthians 12 that "the gospel church" is that historical body that

10. CK, p. 4; cf. CB, p. 373.
11. RGD, pp. 6–7.
12. CSGC, pp. 21f.

. . . comprehends in it the whole collection of those who, in this world, make an orthodox profession of the faith and truth as it is in Jesus. It is the church militant considered in its visibility, as it is looked upon in all its parts and members, through the whole earth, and successively in all the generations.[13]

This visible and militant church in history is not defined according to the purity of its membership but according to its profession of faith. This is why Willard could disagree strongly with the Anabaptists, and still claim that they were frequently godly men "in the main of their profession." While the Lutherans were quite wrong in their understanding of the presence of Christ in the Holy Eucharist, their tradition was part of the gospel church. Although the patristic and medieval church had been covered by a cloud of superstition, still it was the church of Christ that had been covered. Not so, however, with the Deists. Their profession clearly severed them from the revealing God disclosed in Jesus Christ.[14]

The community of the covenant of grace embraces all those who acknowledge the authority of God's Word and receive the "positive institutions" which God in loving freedom ordained for his people's well-being.

The gospel church exists in the world not to serve itself but to live for God and the world of God's creation. Although God could have spread his Word "immediately by his Spirit," or "could have employed the glorious angels in this affair," the fact remains that God invested "this treasure in earthen vessels" by choosing finite and fallible men "to be the ordinary dispensers of this gospel." The community of the covenant of grace holds in sacred trust the prime responsibility for communicating the good news

13. CSGC, p. 12.
14. CB, p. 852.

of God's gracious promise to the world, and the preachment goes out to all within earshot: "the outward discoveries of Christ which are made in the gospel and ordinances, . . . are made to all promiscuously to whom the means of grace are sent, and the great truths which concern Christ and salvation by him are urged upon them." "The invitations of the gospel are to all where the sound of it comes." "The proclamation is to all of what sort soever." [15]

While the community's spokesmen are under obligation "to open and offer this grace to all that hear them," the entire world has not yet been exposed. Simple observation indicates that "the far greater part of mankind have hitherto been strangers to the means of grace, and so out of the way in which the Spirit of God is wont to apply Christ's redemption to men." [16] Within the jurisdiction of Massachusetts, however, it is hard to believe there existed a single soul who had reached the age of accountability who lacked some minimal awareness of the new covenant. In any event, Massachusetts was publicly committed to the proposition that no citizen ought to be deprived of the opportunity of knowing as fully as possible the content of the covenant of grace. According to Willard's reading of the founding of the Bay Colony at least,

> The main errand which brought your fathers into this wilderness, was not only that they might themselves enjoy, but that they might settle for their children, and leave them in full possession of the free, pure, and uncorrupted liberties of the covenant of grace. They have made this profession openly to the world.
>
> . . . and their great care is that religion may not die with them, they would fain that God's covenant might be perpetuated, though they must be removed, and that Christ when

15. FO, pp. 47, 52–54, 130; MM, pp. 251–52; TBM, p. 257.
16. CB, p. 248.

he comes to judgment might here find a church, or churches, that truly serve him.[17]

As part of the civil compact Massachusetts by law required attendance in weekly worship services. Some citizens undoubtedly rejected as false the claim that God had opened a new covenant for fallen humanity. Indeed, some "natural men" saw no need for healing at all, and others held "an obstinate and a malicious hatred of the gospel way of salvation."

> The fouler the stomach, the more nauseous is the physic. When the malady is come to a dangerous crisis, and every symptom bodes a sad and sudden change, men are better pleased with a cheating quack, that dissembleth the disease, and engageth all shall be well, than with an honest and faithful physician, who tells them the distemper is malignant, the issue dubious, and, without the application of some speedy and extraordinary means, desperate. He that will undertake to lay open the true state of degenerous people, by ripping up their sins, displaying their impenitencies, and applying the threatenings of divine displeasure, shall expose himself to the hatred and injurious usage of those for whom he doth this kindness.[18]

And others wanted cheap grace:

> Some there be who are all for gospel preaching, as they please to call it; i.e. nothing but comforts, and consolations by Jesus Christ, and they like not any other preachers but such. But we must remember that consolation is offered too soon to man, if it come before sin is discovered in them.[19]

In Willard's eyes, "the gospel is not properly preached to men till they are prepared for it by the law." The intention of the law, in this context, is focused upon "driving them

17. CK, pp. 117–18.
18. TBM, p. 28; WPTC, pp. 163–64.
19. CB, p. 170.

out of themselves" so that they will put their confidence in Christ. Ministers, therefore, should never preach the law by itself, for that would "drive men to desperation." Rather, "the law ought always to be dispensed with respect to the Mediator." [20]

When the preaching is done well and is heard with sensitivity, the hearer experiences both a "sense of utmost distress, and a discovery of the riches and readiness of Christ for succor; the first of these without the second breeds despair, the second without the first meets with scorn and contempt." [21]

When one declares openly that fullness of life cannot be found within man's natural powers and accepts as true the claim that God's grace alone is sufficient to heal the human heart, then one "owns" the covenant.[22] This transition indicates that one ceases to live in the "wilderness" of the world and comes to be a "visible professor" in "God's vineyard." Between the "visible church and the rest of the world" God raises "a fence" which is precisely the covenant of grace.[23]

Important though this transition is, nothing could be more of a distortion of Willard's theology than to think that this transition is tantamount to the religiously decisive transition from the state of apostasy to the state of grace. Why this is the case becomes obvious as soon as the conditional character of the covenant of grace is examined.

The conditions of the covenant of grace

To be "in" the new covenant, an actual participant "in the visible kingdom of Christ," or a citizen of "God's visible

20. MM, pp. 194–95; LEG, pp. 33–34.
21. MM, p. 194; cf. pp. 102f.
22. CK, pp. 122ff.
23. BFD, entire, especially pp. 6–8, 19; SPE, p. 3.

covenant-people," grants one certain rights and privileges, but basically this status simply opens the *possibility* for healing; it does not provide the *actuality* of God's favor or spiritual health. Being a "fig tree" in "God's vineyard" only means that one acknowledges God's offer and submits to the conditional terms of the new covenant, and now one "must stand or fall according to the conditions of it." [24]

While God's gracious movement towards the human commonwealth is "absolutely free," this does not mean that God's Word is an "absolute promise," for that would entail a decision and commitment on God's part which obliged him, regardless of how man responded. If that were the case, then man's hope would lack a sufficient ground and he would be saddled with an unresolvable perplexity about where he stood with God. Happily, God's restoring love is extended to men in a "covenant promise"; therefore, the people of God "not only have a hope, but it is a grounded hope, and it is grounded in the covenant. Now that ground of hope which flows from the covenant to the party standing engaged to service, is properly from the condition of it." Simply and precisely because the covenant of grace is a covenant is it essential for there to be specified conditions that must be met in order for the promise to be binding: "hence this performance" of the conditional terms on man's part is "the very way to enjoy the performance of the promise" on God's part. [25]

The conditions to be fulfilled are faith and repentance. Formally the new covenant reads—if one believes in God's Christ and repents of living from and for one's self, then God promises to forgive and restore this one; but if these conditions are not met, then this one has forfeited any claim upon God's promise.

24. EP, p. 175; CK, pp. 38, 85; BFD, pp. 28ff.
25. CK, pp. 10, 16; TBM, pp. 223, 436; cf. UI, p. 10; MC, p. 90; DJ, p. 97; CB, pp. 301ff.

Care should be exercised at this point to not misunderstand the type of conditional clause involved. If it is construed in such a way that it becomes an antecedent condition that merits, earns, or deserves the consequential promise, then one is thrown back upon one's own resources. From this inversion "no comfort" can be drawn, for then one is left in "a life of much busyness" where there is an enormous "striving to attain an unattainable legal perfection." That misunderstandings of this sort do occur Willard makes crystal clear:

> There is a legal as well as an evangelical repentance, and it carrieth a plausible show in it, and how many there be that build a false confidence on it, is hard to tell. There is a repentance before faith, which is only preparatory to believing, and hath not faith mixed in it. Nay, there is a repentance that hinders men from believing, and keeps them off from Christ, and they rely upon it as that which gives them title and evidence to salvation, and so turn the gospel covenant into a covenant of works.[26]

Against legalistic distortions of this sort, Willard stresses that the type of dependent condition in the covenant of grace is a "connex-condition." Faith and repentance are simply "the way and means of conveyance, *by* and *in* which God gives the things which are promised, but not for which, and yet *without* which they are not given." (Emphasis added.)[27] Man's faith and obedience do not earn, merit, or deserve God's favor at all; they receive it with thanksgiving:

> There are no other conditions required in the gospel, but what among men are required in order to receiving and being invested with the freest gift that can be. There is nothing but acceptance of this gift, and acknowledgment of the kind-

26. MM, p. 360; SM, p. 69; cf. NS, p. 148.
27. See above, chap. 8, n. 8.

ness of the bestower. Faith is the hand that receiveth it. . . .
And what is our obedience, but our thankfulness to God for
so unspeakable a gift? [28]

In the new covenant God does not require "perfection" as
he does in the old; here "God respects sincerity." [29]

God's grace is freely given; nevertheless, though "there be
never so full a fountain, never so much plenty of living
waters, yet if the man do not drink of them, his thirsty soul
will not be satisfied therewith, but he must perish for all."
It is for this reason that Willard maintains that the abundance of mercies "are exhibited and propounded to us
with an IF." [30]

> It is a grand mistake to think, that there are none in a cove-
> nant with God, but those who are absolutely under the prom-
> ise of salvation. The very notion of a covenant implies a
> dependent condition, to which the privileges of it refer. The
> visible covenant then, thus stands: God offers Christ, and
> salvation by him, in the gospel; tells men, if they believe and
> repent they shall be saved; presents the gospel ordinances as
> means to work faith and repentance in them, and so bring
> them to salvation: they accept the offer professedly, submit to
> the terms, and now they are taken under the covenant, and
> must stand or fall to the conditions of it. When they have
> thus done, they are said to be in God's vineyard.[31]

Rhetorically, then, Willard pushes the conditional character
straight to the core of his proclamation of the gospel:

> Consider the covenant under which you stand, hath its
> threatenings as well as its promises. There are indeed great
> and precious promises held out to all those that are in the
> covenant; but they are also under severe menace; and by

28. TBM, p. 255; cf. DJ, p. 26; CB, pp. 71, 94–95; TBM, pp. 223–
24, 436–37; NS, p. 148.
29. CK, pp. 5–6.
30. FO, p. 29; CK, p. 75.
31. BFD, p. 28.

virtue of their station in the visible church, they are equally related to the one as to the other. Do not forget that the gospel covenant hath its conditions, and accordingly as men are under them, so it speaks to them comfort or terror. It saith, if you believe you shall be saved, but it saith too, if you believe not, you shall be damned. It saith, if you bear fruit you shall be commended, but it also assures you, that if you bear none you shall be condemned. Yea, as it hath better promises, so it hath more sever threatenings than the first covenant [of works] had. Think it not to be enough to say, I am in the covenant [of grace], and so to run away with a carnal confidence, that all is well. But put yourselves upon a thorough search, and inquire what part of the covenant you stand under. There is a vast difference between being under the covenant-promise, and threatening; nothing is more comfortable than the former, nothing more amazing than the latter.[32]

The intense heart-probing (which marked Willard's life as well as his message) is directed to discovering whether man, in the vital center of his self-awareness before God the Almighty Father, has made the crucial transfer of his confidence from his own natural powers to God's Christ alone.

Be then thorough, oh my soul! be not afraid to know the worst by thy self; count it thy happiness to be now undeceived, pursue the business home, bring thy self to the light, and cover nothing from the trial. Let the word of God now determine this great question, and let conscience deal truly and faithfully in laying open thy state before it. Examine thy self, prove thy self, know thy self to the bottom.[33]

If the transition has in fact occurred, then one's heart has cordially closed in with Christ, one has fulfilled the conditional terms, one is now in the religious state of grace, and "God is under the obligations, his word is past for it;

32. BFD, p. 160.
33. SM, p. 60.

pardon, and peace, and glory are now the man's by covenant." [34] If the transition has not occurred, then one stands under the threat, not the promise, and one's religious state remains that of apostasy. One's religious situation *coram deo* in fact is even more vulnerable than those who have never heard the covenant of grace proclaimed in the first place: "Poor heathen have not so much to account for, as a people who are in a visible covenant with God have." "There are none upon the face of the earth that stand upon more dangerous precipices than the children of the covenant." [35]

Regardless of how correct one's behavior is or how exhaustively one studies and accepts as true theologically orthodox beliefs, unless one is internally related to the covenant of grace, one's life-relationship to God remains defined by the covenant of works:

> But others there be who are born under the dispensation of the gospel covenant; who have had this great privilege urged upon them, and been entreated to accept of Christ to be a Mediator for them, and possibly boast of their title to him, but they were never brought over to a cordial closure with him, by a true and living faith, but are still unbelievers; and are therefore, as to their natural estate, under the first covenant [of works].[36]

The difference between these unregenerate Christians and "poor heathen" lies primarily in the fact that those who have "owned" the new covenant already realize that any attempt to secure ultimate fruition within the constitutional order of the old covenant that requires perfection is a lost cause.

Because of the conditional character of the covenant of grace, "there are two sorts of professors in the visible church:

34. BFD, p. 266.
35. CK, pp. 65, 75.
36. CB, p. 317; cf. p. 286; DJ, pp. 16–17.

carnal men, who never experienced the gracious presence of God with them . . . ; and gracious souls, who have been made apprehensive of the love of God, and felt the preciousness of communion with him." [37] Many there are who know the truth of the Christian religion who cannot find it in themselves to accept with their hearts. When they plunge into the depths of self-examination, they do have control of the right criterion but they lack the presence of the Spirit of Christ so that they can surface again with joy. Participants within the gospel church who have "the name, but have not the heart of God's people" are encouraged by Willard to attend prayerfully to the means of grace. Perhaps they too will witness the movement of grace, for the Spirit "is wont to confer it upon us when we are in the faithful use of the means." [38]

The sacramental seals of the covenant of grace

In order to seal the new covenant, sacraments were instituted positively to exhibit the promise in a visible way. What differentiates a sacrament from an ordinary ordinance like preaching and prayer is precisely its visibility or "sensible" character, for a sacramental sign must stand "objectively before our bodily senses" so that we can see, feel, and taste it. In sacramental actions men actually "handle the Word of Life." [39]

The grace of God is truly conveyed through the sacraments, though the "real operation" proceeds not from "any inherent quality" within the sign as such, but totally through "the work of the Holy Spirit, who applies the thing signified, on which the efficacy of these [sacramental signs] doth depend." Because the sacraments are appointed by

37. SD, pp. 6–7.
38. CB, p. 253; BFD, pp. 92–93; cf. MM, pp. 188–90.
39. CB, p. 840; see above, chap. 8, fifth section.

God, instituted by Christ, and empowered by the Holy Spirit, the efficacy of the sacraments likewise is not limited by the state or intention of the one administering them. The objective grace of God in a sacrament exists solely in the mode of the Spirit.[40]

Before the time of Jesus the community of the covenant of grace (Israel) used ceremonies like circumcision to exhibit the promise, but in his kingly office Christ commanded the people of God to practice baptism and observe the Lord's Supper as the sacramental seals operative throughout "the evangelical dispensation of the kingdom of Christ."

Precisely because baptism is a sacrament does it consist of an outward sign and a spiritual signification. Willard holds these two distinguishable but inseparable parts together as against those who place an "absolute necessity" upon the physical form on the one hand, and those who spiritualize baptism away on the other. Whereas the former forget the spiritual intent and object, the latter overlook the sensible character of a sacramental sign.

Washing with water represents the initiation into the community of the covenant of grace, and in Willard's judgment, baptism is a direct substitute for the Jewish rite of circumcision. This parallel is Willard's constitutive argument for baptizing infants, though he conceeds that "a man may be a godly man, and yet be doubtful about infant baptism." [41]

On the manner of baptizing Willard observes that in "Greek classic authors" the term "baptism" denotes both immersion and sprinkling, and he freely admits that during the earliest periods of church history immersion was the more prevalent practice. Nevertheless, as Christianity spread to "the colder regions" sprinkling became the more usual

40. CB, pp. 837, 841, 842.
41. CB, p. 848.

mode, and Willard insists that matters of this sort should be governed "according to the rules of prudence." [42]

Willard's most serious objection against those who reject sprinkling as a legitimate mode of baptism turns not on their understanding of the practice itself but rather on their rigid insistence upon form and their "undue separation" which vitiates "that unity which ought to be in the church of God." [43]

As baptism is the sign of initiation, the Lord's Supper is the sacramental sign of sustenance within the community. It, more than any other act, expresses the "mutual conjugal love" between "Christ and his spouse." [44]

As an outward sign, bread is "aptly suited" to signify the body of our Lord. Its natural connotation as "the staff of life" makes it highly "accommodable to such a significa-tion." As bread is the basic food of man's physical life, so also is Christ the basic food for man's spiritual life. On the "hot dispute of old between the Greek and Latin church" over whether the bread should be leavened or unleavened, Willard argues that both are perfectly acceptable and are matters indifferent, but he advocates leavened bread be-cause it is the common bread of the people.[45]

As bread naturally symbolizes the staff of life, so wine naturally symbolizes the "refreshing and cheering" of life. As wine happifies the body, so also Christ happifies the heart and soul of his people.

> Wine is used in some countries for their drink; and it was more especially liberally made use of at their feasts, weddings, and more free entertainments, being accounted the more no-ble sort of drink.

42. CB, pp. 845–46.
43. CB, p. 855.
44. SM, p. 169.
45. CB, p. 860.

Wine is a cordial, it comforts the heart, recruits the faint-
ing spirits, and greatly refresheth them that drink it, when
laboring of infirmities.

Wine is good to drive away sorrow, and make the man
cheerful. . . . It makes a man merry who was sorrowful.

Wine puts boldness and courage into persons, and drives
away fear, and this it doth by exciting the spirits of activity.

Wine will open the lips, and make them that were silent to
talk.

Wine is used in surgery, to cleanse and purge the wounds
men have gotten.[46]

In each instance Willard finds the parallel with Christ's
work compelling. The efficacious power of the Lord's Supper, nevertheless, does not rest in this natural appropriate-
ness of bread and wine as symbols of the body and blood
of Christ. They become sacramental signs only through
divine appointment. So the crucial question is now posed:
"Surely . . . there is something else here to be met with,
than the naked elements; and what is that but Christ himself? His body and blood?" "But how, or after what manner,
shall I apprehend the presence of Christ *in* and *with* these
outward elements? Doubtless, Christ is in some sort here
according to his human nature. . . ." [47] But how? According to Willard's understanding, Roman Catholics believe

that by the words of consecration the elements are by a
miracle, turned into the real body and blood of Christ, by
transubstantiation; and that the whole essence of these
elements ceaseth, and only the species remain, under which
these are comprehended: and their great plea is for Christ's
express saying, *This is my body,* in which they allow no
trope.[48]

46. SM, pp. 13–16.
47. SM, p. 18.
48. CB, p. 865.

Willard puts this question to himself:

> Shall I believe that the same real humanity of Christ, which was born of the Virgin, is so closely and materially united to the elements, that they are transubstantiated accidents of bread and wine? [49]

Willard's reply contains three levels of argumentation.

> My seeing, my feeling, my smelling, my tasting, tell me, that after the consecration it is still true bread, and true wine.

> My reason assures me, that though his divinity is omnipresent, being infinite, yet his humanity being a creature, is finite, and cannot be in divers places at once.

> And my faith tells me, that he is, in his glorified humanity in heaven, at the right hand of God, and therefore cannot, at the same time, be so here in the sacrament.[50]

The Lutheran theory of consubstantiation, according to Willard, stands in the same situation and is open to the same objections. The metaphorical interpretation of the spiritualizers at the other extreme, however, is also unacceptable to Willard. "Is [the relation between the outward signs and their spiritual signification] merely a metaphorical union? Only a shadow and comparison? Is there nothing here, but only a similitudinary representation of Christ? Is this all I have to do, only to consider what are the nature or virtues of the bread and wine, and so to apply them to Christ by way of resemblance?" Willard tells himself, "not so neither." "The sacrament is . . . more than a bare similitude." "It is an instrument of my communion with Christ, and therefore it must needs bring Christ and my soul together." [51]

Willard's position, which weaves its way between the

49. SM, p. 19.
50. SM, pp. 19–20.
51. CB, p. 865; SM, p. 20.

Scylla of transubstantiation and the Charybdis of a metaphorical reduction, centers on the meaning of "is" in
Christ's words, "This is my body." This statement, according to Willard's hermeneutical method, is a tropological
expression in which the subject and predicate are coupled
together in such a way that "the name of the thing signified
is predicated of the sign." While the body and blood of
Christ are "manifestly exhibited *under* the signs of bread
and wine," they are not to be confused *with* them. They
present Christ sacramentally, that is, in the mode of the
Spirit coming through the visible Word, not in the material
elements themselves. Christ's real presence in the sacrament is a "real spiritual presence," not a "real bodily
presence." [52]

In his meditations on the Lord's Supper, Willard maintains that "this is a great mystery, and none can have a
clear apprehension of it, but those that have the experi-
mental tastes of the reality of it in their participation." [53]
Precisely this participation in the Spirit spells the defining
difference between those who are only externally related
to the covenant of grace and those who are also internally
related by a cordial and living faith.

The presence of the Spirit and the judgment of charity

The pivotal lines of demarcation in Willard's perceptions
of the modes of presence by the Spirit of God are most
readily envisioned through a series of concentric circles.
The outermost limits are composed by the world of God's
creation, which he loves with a "common" love, and which
exists in and through "God's common and universal gov-

52. CB, pp. 863, 865; SM, p. 44.
53. SM, p. 21.

ernment of the world, by which he is intimately present with all creatures. . . ." Within this circle lies a second one which embraces all reasonable creatures or moral agents who exist in and through God's "special and powerful government." At these levels God never withdraws his presence for an instant. Were he to do so the world would collapse into nothingness, or the moral order would dissolve, and this will never happen. God's faithfulness guarantees that. Dramatically put, even in hell itself the divine presence upholds the ontological and moral realms. The "presence of special grace," however, is a third circle within the other two, and at this level the Spirit can withdraw himself, and the Spirit can choose to energize the soul. This is the religious level where the absence or presence of God's Spirit haunts or heals the condition of man.[54]

Again using concentric circles, humanity can be readily sorted out into four basic types of relationships to the Spirit.

First, there are those moral agents who have never been exposed to God's "special grace." These are the heathen who know nothing of the covenant of grace and experience only the common presence of the Spirit.

Second, there are those who have heard and rejected as false the claims of the gospel. These are the "natural men" who either see no need for being cured or who do not believe the prescription is sound. Still they have received the means of preaching and the Spirit has come externally to them.

Third, there are those who have heard the good news, accepted the Christian claim as true, and have "owned" the covenant of grace. These are those who have received the means of preaching and baptism, and consequently have moved from the "wilderness" to "God's vineyard." The

54. MM, pp. 53–54; FO, pp. 59–60.

Spirit ordinarily works powerfully upon them, though not necessarily within them.

Fourth, the inmost circle is reserved for those who have heard the gospel, accepted its claims as true, and have made the transition to cordially closing in with Christ by a living faith that fulfills the conditional terms of the covenant of grace. These are those who have received the means of preaching, baptism and can partake of the Lord's Supper in good faith. Upon these alone has the Spirit descended to burn into their most secret hearts with God's "special love and favor."

None in Willard's Massachusetts, except perhaps a remote Indian, remained in the first circle, and even the second circle does not solicit Willard's concern with anything approaching what the third does, for that is where the children are. Unless these are transformed by the Spirit and enter the fourth circle, all would be lost in the final analysis. The community of the covenant of grace, however, can do no more than present the outward means and prayerfully wait for the Spirit. To move one inwardly is the sole prerogative of the Spirit, and "in the covenant every one stands upon his own bottom." [55] The individual must do his own believing, and loving, and dying.

Whether one has actually made the transition from the third to the fourth circles is something God and the self alone can rightfully know. The community can only accept one's word for it and judge by "charity." Because this is such a sensitive point a series of overlapping quotations is included to register Willard's insistence upon limits— limits which could be easily and harmfully violated.

> No man can infallibly know another's good estate without divine revelation. The differencing notes by which sincerity and hypocrisy are to be distinguished are latent. God only

55. HM, p. 21; CK, p. 71; cf. BFD, p. 228.

knows them certainly. A man may make a great show, and carry it with a great deal of strict preciseness, and yet be rotten within. . . . It is God's alone prerogative to judge the heart.[56]

Hence they should not too easily withdraw communion one from another. It is true, sometimes they that are truly godly, may so fall into sin, and be so remorseless under it, as to be necessarily denied communion with God's people for a season, in a medicinal way, for the helping of their repentance, and bringing them to a kindly sight of, and sorrow for their sin. But to do this, or threaten it upon every occasion of offense, is contrary to that love we are treating of. What great faults did the apostle discover among his Corinthians, and yet he did not for each of these advise the exclusion of such as were guilty, from fellowship with the church.[57]

But then there is a jealousy which fills us with undue suspicions of them; and this is a worm that lies at the root of love and endangers the life of it. This makes us to aggravate all their sins of infirmity, by looking on them through the magnifying glass of prejudice, and to put a sinister interpretation upon their best and most laudable actions as if they proceeded from a false heart. . . . And this is it which makes us to keep a watch upon every word and carriage of theirs, seeking to find advantage against them.[58]

If Christians do always keep their eyes upon the dark side of their brethren, their love will soon wither, and quite wear away. But let us, when we see enough and too much of this, reflect and say, I find this folly in my brother to try my love to him.[59]

Learn hence what need the people of God have, to exercise a great deal of charity one towards another. This consideration, that they are not only liable to temptation, but

56. MC, p. 71.
57. BL, pp. 240–41.
58. BL, p. 259.
59. BL, p. 262.

that Satan is awfully concerned in it, should make us wary
of overcensuring our breathren or charging too heavily upon
them. It requires us to be cautious what animadversions we
make upon their sinful actions. We indeed may and ought to
judge of them as they are, and that by the Word of God.
A sin is not less a sin, because committed by a child of God,
and must be so reputed. But yet there must be a great deal
of charity in exercise, in our particular judgment about it.
And we are to allow them the consideration of being
tempted, and how easily they may be overcome, if God shall
suffer the adversary to prevail over them. We ought to hope
and believe, as far as may be, that they would not allow
themselves in a known sin, and that therefore the enemy hath
imposed upon and deceived them; and accordingly to pity
them, and not to insult over them; to condole, and not to
calumniate them, to afford them an hand to pluck them out,
and not to sink them deeper in the mire of temptation. And
above all, not to lose our charity concerning them, in respect
of their state of grace. No, though they should fall grossly,
and lie too securely under their falls, and that for a considerable time; yea and it may be show too much of a dis-
tempered mind, in their entertaining of the due and just
rebukes that are administered to them. . . . To remember
that we also are of the church militant, engaged in the same
field of war with them, concerned with the same adversaries,
labor under like infirmities, and are exposed to be encoun-
tered like temptations; and if God permits, Satan will not
only soon fall upon us, but also entangle us, and draw us
away with his wiles; and then we shall stand in as much need
of charity and compassion as they do now.[60]

Now, because this relation of true Christians one to another, is built upon their relation to God by the new birth;
and because the new birth is produced by the internal and secret operation of the Spirit of God; and for that reason is not
directly and infallibly to be known by any but God, and the
man himself, who is the subject of it, without immediate

60. CE, pp. 141–42.

revelation. . . . And therefore the highest assurance that we can have of it is that of charity, which argueth from the visible and apparent fruits to the hidden and secret root, and judgeth accordingly; in which, through the great deceitfulness there is in the hearts of men, we may be, and often are mistaken. Nevertheless God hath made it our duty by this rule to reckon and judge of men, and accordingly to love them as brethren, till such time as they do convincingly discover themselves to be strangers to the grace of regeneration. And therefore, the household of faith, or such as do make a good profession of the gospel, and do suitably adorn it in their conversations, are to be reckoned by us as true believers, and children of God, and accordingly to be accounted of, and loved by us as brethen.[61]

Whether the self has endured the "pains and costs" of turning from a project centered somewhere other than the glory of God's kingdom to a living faith in God's Christ is something only God and the self genuinely know. The community can only infer from what is made "visible" in concrete action and make a charitable judgment. When the self has truly turned, though, the "whole man" follows the Spirit into a new kingdom in which the trajectory exhibited in this man's life-relationship to God is anchored in faith, expressed in love, and enjoyed in hope.

61. BL, p. 223.

CHAPTER TEN

The Life of Faith, Love, and Hope

*Now they [God and man] strike hands in an everlast-
ing covenant. All obstacles being removed, the matter
is brought to an upshot, a peace is firmly made, a
covenant signed and sealed; wherein God bindeth
himself in a promise, that eternity, which should have
been spent in executing his wrath upon them, shall be
employed in the entertainment of them with the highest expressions of an infinite love, and nothing shall
ever make a separation between them. . . . And they
on the other hand engage, that by the grace of God,
they will live eternally to his praise, and glorify him
in life, death, and forever. . . . Thus are God and
man atoned, and made one again, all distances removed, all differences buried in oblivion. God hath
cast all their sins behind his back, blotted them out
as a cloud. . . . And God is precious to them, their
hearts are engaged to him, devoted to his praise, and
so fixed in their love to him, that all waters of afflic-
tion cannot extinguish it.*[1]

The paradox of grace

When the Spirit leads the human heart to choose deliberately and to embrace cordially God's Christ, then one

1. CB, p. 310.

experiences a liberating surge of joy, for the war is over and peace dawns within the divine-human community. By turning, man has "cast off the usurped government of other lords" and committed himself to becoming a citizen in God's kingdom. Freed from the tyrannies that crush the human spirit, he is now freed for the creative life where all his powers are shaped by the Spirit towards the end of enjoyment of "complete and unintermixed satisfaction . . . in the highest degree which our natures are able to receive." [2] That is the beatific vision the Spirit has in view as the final destiny of the saint. The Spirit's task here and now is to etch the lineaments of the obediential life of faith, love, and hope on the recalcitrant heart of man so that he can serve the kingdom in perfect freedom.

The communion between God and man created afresh by the transforming presence of the Spirit rests on the union of the believer with Christ. Of all the biblical "similitudes" used to express this mystery, Willard thinks the most adequate is the relationship between husband and wife, for marriage is "a rational union, and is founded, in mutual consent, from whence proceeds that bond by which, they are tied one to the other inseparably." [3] As lovers quarreling over the "frame" of their life together, the Spirit and the self will struggle with each other to the end, but never will they sue for a divorce. Once the conditional terms of the covenant of grace are met, the marriage is sealed into "an everlasting covenant" capable of withstanding any and every assault. The interpersonal relationships and interdependencies are so profound that neither could will to be without the other. Both centers of personal power so interpenetrate each other that their destiny becomes one, but throughout the intertwining process the Spirit remains Lord. Both act, but God is sovereign.

2. CK, p. 61; CP, pp. 137–38; EP, p. 207; CB, pp. 8, 54, 113.
3. CB, p. 430.

Because power flows from two agents in a dynamic inter-play, Willard resorts to paradoxical language to express the truth about the life of faith, love, and hope.

> It may seem a paradox, but it is an evangelical truth, that a Christian must acknowledge that he can do nothing, and yet resolve, and bind himself to do all.

> Though all grace be the free gift of God, and a fruit of his mere bounty, and can no way come within the reach of our merit; yet it is the pleasure of God to command men to buy it, if they will have it.

> . . . there is so much of paradox in these promises, that sense is blundered at them, and carnal reason is run aground at the contemplation of them, and faith only can make true English of them.[4]

Willard's attempt to understand and communicate the mystery of the union of the believer with Christ begins with the foundation laid in the "everlasting covenant" where man's "heart . . . is inwardly principled with saving grace." [5]

Nature and grace

Willard's deepest conviction about the process of healing man's disrupted heart is that God's "grace doth not destroy but rectify nature." [6] For the rebel to become "a new man in Christ," he must receive from the Spirit a "new principle" to capacitate him for participating within the community of faith, love, and hope.

> All acts require a power suitable and sufficient for them; nor can any agent go beyond its ability. No effect can exceed the virtue of its cause.

4. NS, p. 149; HM, p. 21; JMP, p. 2.
5. NS, pp. 135–36.
6. SD, p. 71; cf. CP, p. 89.

> Philosophy tells us, that life-actions require life in the agent. And spiritual actions must derive from a spiritual life; gracious actions must flow from grace. Call this an habit, or a virtue, or a principle; it must be an ability to do these things, which it had not naturally, but must be given it.[7]

While there is "an active principle in him, which may be wrought upon and excited, so as to receive the habits of human sciences, and common morality," human nature alone lacks the power to cross the infinite qualitative distance between nature and the supernatural realm: "there is nothing more than a passive power to receive these supernatural habits of saving grace." To claim that the human condition could be healed and man could "perform true obedience to God" through the native powers ingredient in man's natural endowment would be to "deny godliness." [8]

Even though human nature by itself lacks the ability to effect the transition into the supernatural arena, it can receive the gift(s) which will enable man to perform "spiritual actions" or "gracious actions." (By contrast, anything less than "a cause by counsel" lacks even a passive power to receive the supernatural gift(s) of grace.) The only power sufficient to create new principles and implant them in human nature is omnipotence itself, and that is precisely what God does through the agency of the Spirit: "When the Spirit of God comes to produce this great change in a sinner, he infuseth into him all his sanctifying graces." Gifted to some fallen men is "the image of God" that Adam forfeited: "what else is this sanctification, but the renewing of the image of God in man, which is proper furniture to fit him for the service of God, according to his revealed will." [9]

7. CB, pp. 434–35, 426ff.

8. PT, p. 28; cf. EP, p. 184; TBM, p. 291.

9. FO, p. 133; CB, p. 571; cf. CB, pp. 492–93, 582; MM, p. 349; LEG, p. 29; RMD, p. 147.

The moment of infusion, Willard claims, cannot be determined, for "the habits of grace come in undiscerned." In regard to infants, anyhow, Willard argues that

> We can readily conceive them subjects as well capable of the sanctification of the Spirit, as of natural corruption: though how they should exert acts of faith and repentance, is beyond our conjecture.[10]

At some time, though, the Spirit plants the "seed," nurtures the "root," establishes the "principle," and in this decisive act man is completely *passive*. Although "passive conversion" is "done by the Spirit alone," man is *active* in his "active conversion," namely, that personal process of "exerting and exercising" the graces received. In the healing process itself the Spirit "co-operates with us."[11] Believers live from, in, and for the Spirit, but the participative acts are human actions.

One cardinal difference between the Spirit's implanting the divine image originally in Adam and now in fallen men is that Adam put up no resistance. Here the Spirit must overcome active opposition.

To prepare one for communion, the Spirit discloses through "terrible discoveries" how profoundly one has betrayed one's personal trust. The Spirit's intent in "convicting" one destined for "the everlasting covenant" is to empty the soul, "for as long as a man is full of himself, of the world, of his carnal hopes, of his legal righteousness, there is no room for the Spirit of God." Purging man's heart of "self-sovereignty" through "terrors," however, does nothing more than "terrify, amaze, make afraid." While fear can restrain and empty, it can never turn man's vital center

10. MM, p. 215; TBM, p. 291.
11. FO, p. 131.

towards his proper end. That can be brought about solely through God's love: "the goodness of God is the great motive to true repentance. . . . God wins the soul to himself nextly, not by terrors, but by his benignity. . . . this is that which wins the soul, breaks the heart, encourageth hope, and by this way the Spirit worketh the soul to repentance." [12] Love alone can bend man's heart from his own teleology towards the teleology of Christ's kingdom.

Within these broad poles, furthermore, the Spirit "in his dealings with the souls of men" freely applies himself in his own way so that "the experiences of gracious souls . . . are various on this account."

> In some he makes shorter work by the means, others he holds longer under awakenings, terrors, and etc. Some are drawn to Christ more gently, others more terribly; and all this according as he pleaseth.[13]

Rejecting as normative "any one's particular observation in himself" about his own conversion, Willard explicitly declares that "it will be a great injury to the souls we are concerned with, if we be rigid here." [14]

Willard is firm, though, in insisting that the Spirit, even in the most desperate struggles with ruptured consciences, never violates man's essential being. No distortion of the healing process is more wrong-headed in Willard's eyes than to think that "God deals with men as with sticks and stones, and brute creatures." Because man is a reasonable creature, he is not "a blind or dead thing," his mind is everlastingly active, and his will "must not be forced, but led." In drawing man to himself, God respects absolutely the ontological

12. MM, pp. 176, 205; NS, pp. 139, 144.
13. CB, p. 435.
14. CB, p. 435.

integrity of his own creation; the Spirit proceeds "entirely according to the nature which God had put into us." [15]

The descent of the Spirit into the whole man begins with a persuasion of the mind. Slowly but surely the Spirit "applies himself" through the means of grace so that the understanding is informed of the truth. By "insinuating himself into their minds" the Spirit "works them up to make a deliberate choice, which is not wont to be instantaneous." [16] It takes time to contemplate, to deliberate; it takes courage to undergo self-examination; it takes the Spirit to surface again from these depths with joy because in the Spirit alone can one see and taste God's love for the unlovely.

After the understanding grasps thoroughly "the force of those arguments used by the Spirit" and can "see and approve" through "a rational conviction" the grounds of God's acceptance of a sinner, then the will "willingly" or "voluntarily" reaches out "to embrace the object." [17]

> . . . the truth is thus purchased by a man, when the soul, discerning of a transcendent beauty in it, and persuaded of the incomparable worth of it, prefers it before all other things whatsoever, and parting with everything else, in heart and affection, closeth in with it, and Christ in it, as his only soul satisfying portion.

> . . . at last the will sets its seal to it, chooseth, embraceth, rolls itself upon it.[18]

The recipient of God's grace chooses freely the gift:

> In active conversion, there is a voluntary motion of the soul:
> . . . now a voluntary action is the action of a reasonable creature, applying himself to his object, not upon compulsion, nor by the force of instinct, but by the inclination of

15. MM, pp. 153, 160; CB, p. 443; cf. MM, p. 149; CB, p. 458.
16. CB, p. 441.
17. MM, p. 153.
18. HM, pp. 18–19; DJ, p. 92.

his own mind; so that as he doth it willingly, he also (and therefore) doth it rationally, or upon some apprehended grounds.[19]

Were man's response not voluntary, then God would be denied exactly what he is pursuing, "a free, full, and everlasting choice" by the human "heart." [20]

Analytically the "heart" is equivalent to the "will" of the rational soul, and this power is "the regent in man, and the first mover to every action." When the vital center is turned "the whole man will follow," for directives flow from the command center to the affections to close in with the beloved. The affections consent to being, and the body is moved to express this love in the human world.[21]

In direct parallel to the way in which it covered Adam's natural endowment originally, the renewed "image of God" covers the whole nature of a man whose heart is "inwardly principled with saving grace." [22] (Actually, Willard's argument on the point reverses the progression, for his decisive argument on Adam is an inference from sanctification in the believer.) And it is this new principle of operation that enables a man to serve in the kingdom:

> Created holiness in man, is nothing else but that rectitude
> in his whole nature, and all the powers of it, whereby he is
> enabled and inclined to live and be to the glory of God in
> all things. And from the exerting of this principle do pro-
> ceed all his holy actions.[23]

Although "the image of God" is diffused throughout the entire natural endowment of a believer, it does not follow

19. MM, p. 176.
20. NS, p. 144; cf. DP, pp. 5–6.
21. MM, pp. 157, 203; cf. PT, p. 140; DJ, p. 92; CE, pp. 76–77; WG, p. 29.
22. NS, pp. 135–36.
23. EP, p. 184.

and is not true that this new "body of grace" immediately purges away the old "body of corruption." [24]

> . . . when Christ set up his kingdom in their souls, he put his Spirit upon them but he doth not at once take away all the corruption of their natures.[25]

The purging process in fact is continual throughout the religious state of grace. To the end of his historical career the man of faith encounters opposition within himself; to the end the man of love is engaged in "wrestling and fighting"; to the end the man of hope experiences within himself the conflict between the "Spirit" and the "flesh." [26]

In this context "flesh" does not refer to skin and bones, or corporeality. "Flesh" stands for everything other than the glory of God. And within "the best of God's children here" there is potent resistence to the Spirit's leading: "though the dominion of it [flesh] be broken, the remains of it are strong, active and politic, and it always resists the motions of grace, Gal. 5.17." [27]

It is "a gross delusion," therefore, for people to think that "if they could get into Christ, they should be out of the gunshot of temptation, and full of ease and tranquillity." While such a persuasion is "no uncommon mistake," Willard argues that it flies in the face of both "the unfailing observation and experience of the people of God in all ages" and "the infallible testimony of Scripture." [28]

According to Willard, no Christian who "hath any intimate acquaintance with himself" would disagree with the claim that never in this life could a man be transported

24. PPRM, p. 119.
25. TBM, p. 499.
26. MC, p. 19; cf. CB, pp. 492–95.
27. TBM, pp. 102, 498–500.
28. CE, p. 148; HG, p. 1; cf. TBM, p. 362; CB, p. 314.

into glory where all alienation and hostility are overcome.[29] The classical biblical passage Willard uses repeatedly to reinforce the point that "the true Christian is in his way, travelling out of his far country, and he cannot sit still till he be gotten to heaven," is Romans 7. The apostle Paul, according to Willard's exegesis, was not referring here to some inner conflict prior to his becoming a man in Christ, but rather to the vividly present "conflict between grace and corruption in him, as the whole tenor of his expressions doth evince. . . . It was the mixture which he experienced of sinful corruption with his grace which discovered him not as yet arrived at full perfection." [30]

By insisting that the Christian man is always a pilgrim on his way towards completion and never arrives at perfection in this life, Willard calls attention to the repeated need for the presence of the Spirit to interpret the meaning of the struggle. Not for a moment can the wayfaring warrior stand by himself without the strength of God's Spirit. But the man in Christ, no matter how grievously he succumbs to clamorous impulses or drifts into reluctancy, will never lose "the image of God," not because of some creaturely strength inherent in him but solely because "the power of God . . . keeps it alive." Once the human heart is "made fit to deal with God," then regardless of "whatever shakings it may have," it remains like "the needle in the compass" that "never rests till it comes to point directly to its pole-star." [31] An adopted son in Christ's kingdom will never be abandoned by the Spirit, though the Spirit will continuously lead him into situations where he must rely absolutely upon

29. WG, p. 51; cf. CE, 35; CB, pp. 337, 348; CR, p. 104.
30. MM, p. 279; EP, p. 201; cf. PPRM, p. 119; BFD, p. 72; MC, p. 17; DJ, pp. 23, 69, 110; MW, p. 23; TBM, pp. 79ff, 102, 489, 498f, 547; FO, p. 152; RAD, p. 10; CE, entire, especially pp. 22–26, 35, 137–38, 201; BRGK, p. 17; SM, p. 70; CB, p. 280.
31. CE, p. 30; NS, pp. 135–36.

the Spirit. This dependency is the pilgrim's strength, and properly to understand it takes Willard into an analysis of the virtues of faith, love, and hope.

Although these three supernatural virtues are analytically distinct, Willard insists on the point that they are actually inseparable from each other, for every moment of true obedience involves all three. And each is correlated to distinct yet inseparable "graces" in Willard's theology. Programmatically, faith answers the grace of justification, love follows sanctification, and hope looks forward to glorification. Together these graces form the principle of grace, or "the image of God," and when viewed in their unity, Willard argues that the Spirit infuses them "all together" at the very "instant in which God converts him." "There is therefore no order in the production of these saving qualities in the soul, but they come in all at once." [32] Nevertheless, the *degree* of presence is not constant, for in regard to sanctification and glorification (but not justification) the gifts are present "inchoatively," not "fully." And there is a "succession . . . in the apprehension of the believer, who doth not immediately discern all of them." [33]

The diagram opposite exhibits the tension within the Christian life between the integrating power of the renewed image of God (Spirit) and the disintegrating power of corruption remaining within the believer (flesh, or the old Adam), throughout his historical career as a recipient of the graces of justification, sanctification, and glorification.

Justification by faith

Whenever a man becomes a new creature in Christ, he does not stop rebelling, for the old Adam lives on within

32. MM, pp. 315–16, 153, 349; FO, p. 133; RMD, p. 147; CB, p. 571; TBM, p. 109.
33. LEG, p. 29; MM, pp. 316–17.

Diagram of the Shape of the Christian Life

Spirit: The Image of God

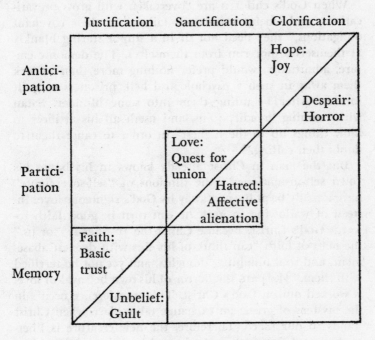

Flesh: The Image of Sin

his breast. Nevertheless, the man who has been led by the Spirit "to adventure his soul upon God" [34] is now freed from the tyranny of his guilty past, and freed for aceptance of himself. No longer does he suffer from the need to deny his guilt, no longer is he compelled to go through the motions of trying to justify himself, no longer does he have to pretend that he can escape from an uneasy conscience.

When God's children are "overtaken with gross prevarications, and woeful scandalous failures in their covenant obligations," they need not sit in a stupor staring blankly at themselves, nor run from themselves. The demonic empire, admittedly, would prefer nothing more than to lock them away in such a psychological hell, prisoners of guilt forever. After beguiling them into some blunder, Satan with cunning "readily joins, and useth all his artifices to blow things up to the highest" in order to cause them to doubt their calling.[35]

But the man in Christ already knows in his bones his "own self-insufficiency"; the illusions of "self-sovereignty" have already been burned away by God's righteous love. Instead of wallowing in guilt he can turn in good faith towards God's Christ. Because Chirst the Justifier is "for us," the man of faith "can think of his sins with deepest abasement, and soul humbling thoughts, and yet not be terrified with them." His past, the horror of his own betrayal of love, is worked out on God's Christ. This transference occurs in the mystery of grace; an exchange takes place when Christ stands in our place. Therefore, the new creature is liberated to make a good confession without being "afraid of being rejected." [36] In faith the heart hears the word of forgiveness:

34. MM, pp. 203–04.
35. CR, p. 104; MRL, p. 22.
36. TBM, p. 15; RAD, p. 35.

> Your follies shall not be laid to your charge, your iniquities
> shall be blotted out of his book of remembrances, sunk down
> as a mill-stone in the depths of the sea, buried in a grave of
> everlasting oblivion.[37]

Daily the pilgrim must reach for "new forgiveness," daily
the warrior must turn in faith for a "pardon," daily the
saint must rise again through "repentance." [38]

On any given day, of course, his faith may be so weak
that the best he can do is utter, "Lord I believe, help mine
unbelief." Willard is of the persuasion that no man is so
established that his faith is "unshaken and never faulters"
during his pilgrimage:

> I am satisfied that there is a mixture of doubting with the
> strongest faith here; and that the greatest assurance in this
> life, is not out of the reach of being shaken in an hour of
> temptation.[39]

Nevertheless, even when an adopted son in God's kingdom
is stumbling in doubtful uncertainty, the Spirit will never
forsake him. "The light of faith," [40] once truly lit, never
will dim all the way out, not because of some inherent
power in the believer, but solely because that light is a gift
from God and the Justifier is everlastingly "for us."

On other days, too, the pilgrim will be trapped in spiritual pride: "Now there is a pride which is very apt to arise
in us, which would make us reckon ourselves to be self
dependent; and hereby self is exalted, and God is dis-
honoured; and we are apt to persuade ourselves that we are
able to serve God, and persevere in that service, by the
strength of grace received," that is, received in some previ-

37. CK, p. 96.
38. EP, p. 204; MM, p. 279; CE, p. 200.
39. SM, pp. 50, 66–67; CE, pp. 201, 240.
40. CB, p. 453.

ous moment, not the present. The Spirit is not such an
absent-hearted lover that he will tolerate for long such out-
rageous distance in the heart of God's children. They will
soon experience a rebuff that "curbs in our pride, and lofty
opinion of ourselves, and makes us freely to confess, that all
our security for eternal life depends upon him alone." [41]

With this insistence on the constant and continual dependency of the believer upon Christ, Willard registers the
fact that it is "not our faith" that justifies and pardons us.
That would be a grotesque involution of the meaning of
justification by faith.

> Faith doth not justify us, as it hath any worth or merit of
> its own in it, to deserve or earn justification for us. . . . But
> in the process of gospel justification, it is Christ's righteous-
> ness which stands to answer in the room of ours, and not our
> faith: So that the merit of our justification is in the object,
> viz. Christ, and not in the act of faith.[42]

> This faith hath Christ for its object, on whom it entirely
> relies for salvation. . . . It centers upon Christ as the ob-
> ject that is therein revealed, and offered in the promise, on
> whom it placeth its whole dependence for life and salva-
> tion.[43]

Man's faith is precisely that act in which he moves out of
himself, completely surrenders reliance upon himself, and
utterly confides in God's Christ who alone exercises power
sufficient to overcome the guilt of man's past. Faith is "the
bond" of union through which the transference takes
place.[44]

Were one satisfied with only the virtue of faith, however,
one would have trifled with God's forgiveness. Mindless
piety that seeks a pardon for sin, without aiming at a purg-

41. CE, pp. 133–34; cf. CB, p. 395.
42. DJ, pp. 94–96.
43. MRL, p. 22.
44. CP, p. 13; DJ, pp. 81–90; FO, p. 30.

ing of sin within the heart, banks on cheap grace and trivializes the relationship between man and God. The authentic act of faith terminates in God's Christ, whose Spirit leads the pilgrim out into the world. Walking by faith, the adopted son in God's kingdom serves through love.[45]

Love and the beauty of holiness

As a citizen in God's kingdom the pilgrim still witnesses within himself the poisoning presence of hatred. The old Adam is still potent. Nevertheless, the new man's vital center is no longer enslaved by hostility and numbness. The weightless void is filled with a new higher principle of action that frees him for loving the really open possibilities of being. As in faith one receives Christ, so in love one serves him. Man's affective life answers the law of God's kingdom because God's love "attracts a reciprocal love from the sinner." "It is the loveliness of the object that attracts our love to it." [46]

When God's people recoil in anger because the work of their hands "is blasted, and ends in frustration, which joins vanity and vexation together," [47] the satanic spirit strikes for their loyalty and love, hoping to carry them off into hatred, the prime alienating affection. Instead of withdrawing love, instead of nursing an affective alienation from the world of God's creation, however, the believer can turn towards God's Christ. Because Christ the Sanctifier is "in us," the new man can pursue a "closing" with God's commands.

Love in us, is an affection leading us in pursuit after union to the object of it, in order to our having intimate com-

45. DJ, pp. 106–07; EP, p. 181; FO, p. 99.
46. CB, p. 113; PPRM, p. 106; MM, p. 314; WG, p. 37; cf. CP, pp. 42–44.
47. CB, p. 226.

munion with it; for love is a closing affection, and carrieth us forth after that which we love. That which attracts our love to it, is the goodness which we apprehend to be in the object of it, which renders it a thing lovely.[48]

Because the Sanctifier is "in us," we are "enabled" to love appropriately and spontaneously. Man now can "participate in," and "be delighted with," the law of his own being which points towards God's glory in all things.[49] Because the Spirit is at work within the heart, freeing the heart from the "pollution" of hatred and liberating the heart for the promise of love, believers see and taste the beauty of holiness and wholeness in and for itself.

The affections are the instruments of the will, by which it exerts itself in the imperate actions, and is therefore to be judged of by them. They are the feet of the soul, which carry it to or from the object which it hath either chosen or rejected, and are accordingly signals of those elicit actions. Where then our love is exerted and exercised about anything, it is a witness that we have chosen that thing, upon an high esteem of, and value for it. For this election being an act of a cause by counsel, it argues, that the soul hath discovered that in the law, which hath satisfied him of the worth and excellence of it, for which it hath rationally given it the preference to every other thing. . . . And this choice is not made on the account of any external or adventitious advantages which he apprehends that he may gain by his obedience, which often allures hypocrites to a temporary compliance, and they are pleased in it, as long as that lasts, but from the intrinsical goodness and worth of the law, which they are persuaded of, and can testify for it.[50]

The Spirit alone can work this "substantial change" in the heart of man so that new men in Christ become "partakers

48. LP, p. 9.
49. LEG, pp. 28–29; TBM, p. 485; EP, p. 182.
50. CB, p. 582.

of the divine nature." As rebellion against the natural moral law commences with a misjudgment of the goodness of being, so the Spirit sanctifies the soul so that it can see the truth of being and obey spontaneously. This affective turning of the whole man towards being is a homecoming "to the natural inclination of the reasonable creature." [51] No longer is God's law of love viewed as an external imposition —from the inside out man can now lovingly serve.

As long as the pilgrim is on his way "another law" within him quarrels with the law of love. In Willard's technical language, "Sanctification . . . is gradual, and not completed at once." [52] But once the eye of the soul has seen, truly seen, the coming glory, the heart will never stop desiring it with "eager longing," hoping for the day when love so interpenetrates the beloved that the soul is filled "with delight and this is properly joy." [53] Serving through love, the adopted son in God's kingdom lives in hope.

The hope of glory

Although the pilgrim receives God's Christ in faith and serves God's kingdom in love, he still is vulnerable to despair as he looks towards the future. Darkness is still present and the old Adam within him still casts doubt upon all paths into the unknown. Nevertheless, the vanity of trying to secure the future through his own resources has already been exposed, and God's Spirit is now at work freeing him for "running with all cheerfulness the race of God's commandments." [54]

So when anxiety grips his heart and Satan lures him into cursing the darkness, the new man in Christ does not need

51. DJ, p. 14; HE, pp. 5–6; CP, p. 23; CB, p. 585.
52. CE, pp. 35–36.
53. CB, pp. 512; cf. 744.
54. CB, p. 113; cf. CP, pp. 42–44.

to remain bogged down in the bottomless pit of despair. Because Christ the Glorifier is "with us," the people of God are upheld even in the midst of perplexing uncertainties by "an hope that shall not make ashamed." [55]

Despair of doing good, is that which enervates the spirits, and puts a damp upon all activity, yea makes men to cast off all endeavors: whereas on the other hand, hope oils the wheels, warms the heart and gives activity to compassion.

Hope is the very life of endeavor; what men despair of they will never attempt to compass; but where there are any sparklings of hope, they will push men on to seek their help. [56]

The believer obviously does not hope in himself. That would be a monstrous perversion: "And do I resolve all my hopes into him [Christ], and not into my repentance?" Hope that is anchored in the covenant moves out to the Lord, "believing that he who hath begun a good work for you will perfect it in you." [57] Because the Glorifier is "with us," the pilgrim is never alone on his way towards his final destiny.

While even the best of believers must struggle with temptation and surely will fall repeatedly, God's children are sustained in their spiritual warfare by their realization that the God of their hope will be faithful to his word of promise and complete his design for the created world by carrying those in the state of grace into glory. In the midst of every adversity the joy of anticipated victory already floods the believer's self-awareness. In a remarkable series of rhetorical questions, Willard spells out the "child's portion":

55. CB, p. 228; cf. MM, p. 352.
56. BFD, pp. 229–300; CB, p. 249.
57. SM, p. 73; CR, p. 165; cf. TBM, p. 553.

Who, but he that enjoys it, can declare what an happiness it is to enjoy peace with God, and fellowship with Christ, assurance of his love, and consolation of his spirit? Who, but he that hath felt it, can tell what it is to have the love of God shed abroad in his heart, and in his soul to hear the sweet voice of pardon, and promises of glory? to lie all night in the bosom of Christ, and have his left hand underneath his head, and his right hand embracing of him? [58]

These foretastes of glory, however, "are but drops, and rivulets which come in pipes, and little portions" compared to the coming time when the adopted sons of the kingdom shall "dwell at the fountain, and swim for ever in those bankless, and bottomless oceans of glory." [59] The religious state of glory, or "the beatifical vision," is a state of "perfect happiness" in which there is "a full freedom from all evil, and an entire fruition of all good." [60]

All streams do naturally lead down to the ocean; and all divine truths do as certainly carry us home to God himself, who is the essential truth. As truth comes from God, so it leads back to God.[61]

Only beyond this life, when there will be a "perfect closure of the faculty with the object," will the believer enjoy "complete and unintermixed satisfaction . . . in the highest degree which our natures are able to receive." "But till all the reachings of the soul are gratified, till all its appetites are filled, it cannot rest; it will be in motion as long as it feels any want." [62] Finally home, the pilgrim can rest, for then his natural desires will be fully satisfied, all alienation overcome, and he will no longer feel within his heart any

58. CP, pp. 69–70.
59. CP, p. 70; cf. CB, pp. 113, 534, 556–58; MM, pp. 351–52.
60. CB, pp. 7, 666; CE, p. 137.
61. HM, p. 81.
62. CP, pp. 137–38.

"want." "When we come there we shall sin no more, nor have any dregs of pollution abiding in us, but be entirely conformed to the image of God." [63]

The degree of "true felicity" a new creature in Christ possesses here and now is measured by the degree to which he has internalized "the image of God" and brought his intentions and actions into "conformity to Christ." [64] In this life the transforming process is never finished; nevertheless, once the Spirit leads a man to become internally related to the covenant of grace so that he is engrafted into Christ, then that man's life-relationship to God is no longer defined by the religious state of apostasy in which his existence is organized by "the image of Sin." Even now he begins to participate in a new life that is integrated by "the image of God." Jesus Christ is now the pattern shaping his existence in the religious state of grace, a pattern that promises completion for man's essential being when the pilgrim is brought to his final destiny in the state of glory. As the rational soul is the form of man as man, so Jesus Christ is the form of man as believer. Because the principle of operation present in Christ carries all of man's natural powers into a higher integration, the man of faith, love, and hope experiences within himself a quickening of joy as he reaches out to embrace his new life in Jesus Christ, the God-man Mediator.

63. EP, pp. 206–07; CB, pp. 8, 54, 113, 281, 338f.
64. CP, pp. 112–23, 127; cf. HE, pp. 5–6.

CHAPTER ELEVEN

Jesus Christ: The God-Man Mediator

It was therefore fit and necessary, that he [Jesus Christ] should be humbled. How else could he answer the law for us, in which he must be subjected to the law, fulfil the righteousness of it, pay our debts, and bear our penalties, satisfy for our offences, and purchase for us, all the good needful to make us happy? If he do not all this, he cannot be our Redeemer; and he could not do this, unless he were humbled. . . . It was no less fit, that after he had humbled himself he should be exalted. For it became him, that having discharged all that he undertook as Mediator, he should have an acquittance; that having merited, he should be rewarded; having purchased, he should be put in possession; so that it might appear that the work was done, that justice had taken up satisfied in it. Our surety had not done his work, till he hath taken up our bonds, and gotten full acquittances for us. In sum, Christ stood as a public person for us. He must therefore be humbled, because we deserved to be brought low. He must be made a curse for us, because we were accursed. And he must be exalted, that so he might bring us to glory.[1]

1. CB, pp. 351–52.

The mission of Jesus Christ

God's love is the only power sufficient to free men from
their anxious revolt and for spontaneous and joyful obedience to God's intention for the divine-human community.
That is the central, organizing claim in Willard's understanding of man's recovery of wholeness. The *structure* of
this divine love is exhibited in the constitutional order of
the covenant of grace. The *application* of this divine love
upon and within the human heart is the work of God the
Spirit. And the *revelation* of this divine love reaches its
clearest and deepest definition in the historical career of
God the Son, for in his obedience Jesus Christ identifies so
intimately with man's broken condition that he takes the
train of evil consequences flowing from man's rebellion
into himself, disclosing in his sacrificial death the extent of
God's reaching out to restore men to their inheritance in
God's kingdom.

Willard's reflection upon what Jesus Christ does and
who he is moves in the realm of mystery, a realm illumined
by "the light of faith." [2] Nothing Willard knows through
"the light of nature" is left behind, though. As grace does
not destroy but fulfills nature, so faith does not violate but
completes reason. The substantive issue at this point in
his "Systematical Divinity" turns on the way he resolves
the tensions between the demands of justice (knowable by
reason through the light of nature) and the promises of
love (received in the knowledge of faith).

Grace is never cheap in Willard's thought: "More cost
must be laid out upon him [fallen man] to make him a
vessel of glory, and fit him up for his Master's use, than
to have made a new world." [3] Jesus Christ is God's payment

2. CB, pp. 290, 293–95, 429.
3. CK, p. 58.

of that cost "and by doing and dying he made way for
grace to triumph." [4] The triumph of grace is the end for
which the Son of God humbled himself and took the form
of the servant.

The Lord as servant

Obedience even unto death on the cross is the appropriate
culmination of Jesus' historical career, for the form of the
servant is present from the beginning. The circumstances
of his birth introduce the pattern of humiliation that Willard discovers throughout the life of Jesus Christ. In Beth-
lehem "the huffing and swaggering blades of the place
take up and command all the entertainment" so that Mary
is reduced to delivering the Prince of Glory in "a nasty
hole." [5] Willard's portrait of Jesus as a young man reveals
a proper Puritan who acknowledged his subjection to his
parents by keeping "a due distance" and "willingly, readily,
cheerfully" obeying their commands. While growing up
Jesus worked at a trade, too: "Labor in some honest calling
is part of man's duty; commanded in the moral law."
Therefore, Jesus "humbleth himself to live by his hands."
As a carpenter he eked out a meager yet dignified existence
through "what he got by industry." [6]

Willard's concern with the servant motif, however, presses
beyond the exemplary domestic virtues in Jesus' "private
life." Of vastly greater moment is his "public service." [7]

Within the institutional structure of Israel's tradition
public service was available through the three "distinct
offices" of prophet, priest, and king. In order for Jesus
to mediate effectively between God and man, Willard

4. CB, p. 264.
5. CB, p. 357.
6. CB, pp. 358–63.
7. CB, p. 358.

argues that it was imperative for him to exercise the functions of all three of these separate yet mutually interdependent public offices.[8]

Jesus was first called into the public domain as a prophet and he carried out the "function" of that particular investiture with superlative style.[9] As a teacher he was not concerned with teaching men "a trade" or even the ways and means of being civilized.[10] Important though these educational goals are, one does not need a prophetic revelation to achieve them. In his teachings Jesus went beyond those matters that can be educed from the principles inherent in human nature to proclaim "the good will of God to fallen man." "The free grace of God" is the only truth sufficient for overcoming the "horrible havoc" sin has introduced in man's mind.[11]

Jesus was not the first prophet to address "our ignorance of the way of peace," [12] yet he "exceeds all the prophets that ever were in the church," for their authority is derivative while his lies within himself. They use the prophetic form, "Hear ye the Word of the Lord," while he is in fact the Word of God in human flesh. In the face of the intractable spirit of man's deceitful heart, many a prophet of Israel sulks, and "if they cannot beat it into us" they scornfully call down upon our heads the wrath of an angry God. Jesus, though, is different. "He is an incomparable prophet," who embodies the message he proclaims.

> He is willing to take pains with us, wait upon us, and follow us with line upon line, and precept upon precept; to teach us a little at one time, and a little at another, according to our bearing. He is willing to speak to us in our

8. CB, pp. 321–23.
9. CB, p. 324.
10. CB, p. 328.
11. CB, pp. 327, 370–71.
12. CB, p. 322.

own language, and accommodate his doctrine to our capacities, and not to upbraid us.

And the manner [of his teachings] was suitable to the matter; gracious words, sweet and alluring rhetoric, heart melting arguments. He had the very art of persuading, and stealing into men's souls.[13]

He who is the Word of God takes the form of the servant to show men from the inside out the meaning of God's love.

Knowing the truth and doing it, however, are two quite different operations. According to Willard's own experience, "a natural man may understand the grammatical and logical meaning of gospel theorems" and still not "see into the mystery of them." The "divine beauty sending its rays" through the teachings of Jesus will be missed unless men have eyes to see.[14] Necessary though it is that the understanding be enlightened, enlightenment alone is insufficient, for the will of man's rational soul must also be turned and empowered to love. Jesus carries out that particular function through his kingly office.

Jesus was not the first person to hold the powers and privileges of the office of king, yet Willard claims that Jesus surpasses "all earthly potentates" because his mastery of the human good is eternal, unshakable, and personal. Anointed king by divine appointment, Jesus' dominion encompasses not only the entire range of the created world, as his miracles attest,[15] but more especially it reaches into the secret terrain of man's most personal interiority and there lays claim upon man's loyalties. Where "terrestrial" kingdoms, "though never so absolute in their government, have only a command over men's bodies and estate," the mediatorial kingdom of Jesus Christ is "spiritual" and

13. CB, pp. 328–29, 371.
14. CB, pp. 326, 327.
15. CB, pp. 371–72.

therefore "Christ's jurisdiction extends to the heart, and rules over the conscience." [16]

He who is the very principle of ultimate sovereignty, moreover, knows full well that "absolute and arbitrary government is among men, no better then tyranny." [17] Even though he "hath an absolute dominion as God," he does not flaunt his prerogative but takes the form of a servant and voluntarily submits to "the legal process" of the human world.

> He was an anointed king, and yet would be a servant. He was judge of the world, and yet would stand at man's bar, and there be arraigned, condemned and executed.[18]

By serving human needs Jesus shows the power of God's love. Under his command man's conscience no longer stifles and kills the human spirit. By securing "spiritual peace" within man's conscience, Jesus opens the way for "rebels and enemies" to become "free and voluntary subjects," citizens of the realm. In his kingly office Jesus "takes the obstinacy out of their hearts, and cures the enmity that is in their wills" by empowering them to respond appropriately to God's law of love.[19]

For God and man to be reconciled to each other, however, Jesus needs to do more than enlighten the mind through his prophetic office and empower the will through his kingly office. Deeper than man's "ignorance" and "impotency" lies his affective "alienation from God." [20] Man's betrayal of his pledged word has contaminated the moral entity established by God and Adam with so many suspicions and jealousies that only an atonement can restore

16. CB, pp. 343, 349–50.
17. CB, pp. 345, 350.
18. CB, p. 353.
19. CB, pp. 344–45.
20. CB, p. 322.

communion between the antagonists. In his priestly office Jesus Christ accomplishes this mutual reconciliation, according to Willard, by standing "in our place" and offering up himself as a vicarious sacrifice.

The vicarious sacrifice

The death and resurrection of Jesus Christ is the mirror in which Willard sees the profoundest depths of "God's heart," [21] for in offering himself up as a vicarious sacrifice Jesus takes away man's guilt in the presence of God, and in triumphing over death he shows forth God's love in the presence of man.

Because of this "exchange" [22] of place in which "all the guilt which was before ours, now became his, and was translated on him," [23] a man can look steadily into the most secret recesses of his consciousness without fear of rejection. No longer does he need to run from what he has become or fall away with self-loathing when he is forced to face what he really is. When the Spirit applies the grace achieved through the redemptive exchange in Jesus Christ, a man is brought to see the truth in love.

God now reveals that he is fully reconciled to, and at peace with him; and all former distances and alienations of heart are wholly taken away. He is no more angry, nor will any more condemn him.

. . . God gives himself to the sinner to be his, and takes him to himself, makes himself to be his portion, and bequeaths himself to him, and receives him into arms of mercy, making him his peculiar treasure and jewel.[24]

21. CB, p. 266.
22. DJ, p. 59; SM, pp. 45–46; CB, pp. 282, 311–12, 332–34; CR, p. 143.
23. CB, p. 392.
24. MM, pp. 312–13.

But the price of admission to this vision of God's transforming love is a thorough awareness that one's personal
betrayals contribute directly to the suffering of Jesus
Christ.

Jesus' agony was as intense as his death was real, for
Willard believes "that God must make the way to his
being reconciled to us, through the heart of his own Son,
and he must die, that we may live; he must pay the whole
price, that we may be discharged; he must bear the full
weight of wrath, that we may escape it." [25] The intensity
of Jesus' suffering, in Willard's perspective, did not arise
primarily from the contempt the "rascally multitude"
poured on him, nor from the fact that he was crucified "as
a public enemy both to church and state." [26] Bitter though
it was that he stood wrongly condemned through "a legal
process" that involved an "ecclesiastical council" as well
as a "civil magistrate," [27] the intense quality of his death
arose from his "voluntary" embrace of "the penalty of our
sins." "It was not the malice of Satan, nor the spite of the
Jews, that properly brought him to his cross, but the sin
of man." [28] And in opening his most personal being to
man's sinful condition, Jesus realized in his inmost self
that he would have "to undergo the whole essence of the
penalty denounced by God against sin." [29]

In the garden of Gethsemane, when Jesus felt what the
hideous quality of man's sin would do to him, "a conflict,
strife, or combat" was released within Jesus' soul that was
so acute that Willard calls it a "spiritual death." Gone was
the "joy and delight" he had experienced in God's presence; "now, sorrow, sadness, and soul-heaviness fell upon

25. CB, p. 383.
26. CB, pp. 389–90.
27. CB, p. 392.
28. CB, p. 381.
29. SM, p. 97; cf. CB, p. 384.

him, and had liked to have killed him." [30] What "dreadfully amazed" Jesus throughout his suffering was not so much his bodily death but that he was forsaken "at God's judgment seat." [31]

> God did not spare him, but made his soul an offering for sin, cast him into the floods of vengeance, and all the billows of his wrath past over him, made him a curse, and filled him with all his shafts cutting him off from the earth, not leaving him, till the law had its full satisfaction upon him to the utmost of its demands: his Father, all this while carrying it towards him as an enemy, hiding up from him every beam of his favor, filling him with a sense of the dismal effects of that holy wrath of his, which he had declared against sin; which are in themselves inexpressible, unconceivable.[32]

And when Jesus of Nazareth finally died, "it was no fictitious death that he underwent." Death snapped "the union of his blessed soul and body" and immediately his "reasonable soul" lost control over its expressive organs.

> His merciful hands moved not; his compassionate eyes were closed; his attentive ears were stopped; his feet that were wont to travel for the good of sinners were shackled with the fetters of death; his gracious tongue was now tied, and his sweet lips were now shut up.[33]

Just like any other man his body now became "an ignominious spectacle" in "death's triumph over him."

By raising Jesus from the dead, Willard believes God unequivocally attests to the sufficiency of "our high priest's" obedience in paying "a full proportionable price to the full demands of what justice could possibly make." Because

30. CB, pp. 384–86.
31. CB, p. 397; cf. p. 283.
32. SM, pp. 97–98; cf. 12, 15, 45, 93, 96.
33. CB, pp. 403–04.

the exchange of place in the vicarious sacrifice takes away man's guilt, justice no longer "stops up the way of mercy." [34] Through his work Jesus Christ opens the fountain of divine grace so that God's forgiving love can now flow forth without violating "God's honor." For Willard the resurrection validates the belief that within the divine life justice and love, righteousness and mercy "entertain each other with mutual embraces of perfect amity." [35]

This "sweet consent" between God's attributes is made known to and reflected by all those whom "the second Adam" represents as "a public person." [36]

The public person of the second Adam

The baseline of Willard's treatment of the person of Jesus Christ is drawn in his assertion that "had Christ been mere man, he had been too weak; had he been only God and not man, he had not been fit to be our Redeemer." [37] In order for Jesus Christ to be the Mediator who overcomes the alienation and opens a friendship between God and man, Willard argues that it is necessary for Jesus to be both divine and human. All that he does in his mediatorial offices of prophet, priest, and king are the actions of an individual person who unites within himself "two natures infinitely disproportionable in themselves" so that properly he is a "God-man."

In no way does the claim that all the actions of the incarnate Lord are "theandrical" involve a collapse between the two natures so that one is absorbed into the other. Throughout his humiliation in history and exaltation in

---

34. CB, pp. 283, 311; cf. 277, 331.
35. CK, p. 17; cf. MRL, p. 26; TBM, p. 254; CB, pp. 304, 308, 340; CR, p. 97.
36. CK, p. 3; CB, pp. 351–52.
37. CB, p. 290.

glory, Jesus Christ retains "two distinct" understandings and wills. Nevertheless, his human and divine natures are "conjoined" in his personal acts in so intimate a manner that Willard maintains that "this man is God." [38]

Willard does not pretend to "comprehend" the incarnation: "the causes are too mysterious for us, and so our understanding is non-plust in the contemplation of it." But in "the light of faith" the mind of man can "apprehend" the "effect" of the incarnation.[39] This "effect" becomes manifest in the resurrection, and from that perspective Willard traces the union of the divine presence "veiled" in human form back through the ministry of Jesus of Nazareth to the very moment of his conception in the womb of the Virgin Mary.

In discussing Jesus' conception and birth Willard cautions against putting credence in the numerous legendary accretions to the biblical narratives, claiming that "so many of them are plainly ridiculous, and have neither footing for them in Scripture, nor any usefulness in divinity." And Willard does everything but explicitly deny Mary's perpetual virginity, accusing some Protestants of being "over-superstitious" in this regard, and even suggesting that if Jesus did have blood brothers then it "might be a further testimony of his [Jesus'] love to mankind." And it certainly is Willard's opinion that Mary had "not arrived at spotless perfection, but had the stain and pollution" of original sin while she was carrying Jesus.[40]

In regard to "the formation, animation, and ripening" of the fetus in Mary's womb, "nothing extraordinary" transpired either. Willard rejects as "an old dream" the gnostic notion that "the body of Christ was formed in heaven, of heavenly matter, and was only miraculously put

38. CB, pp. 294–95; CE, p. 82.
39. CB, pp. 290, 293–95, 429.
40. CB, pp. 299, 357.

into the Virgin's womb, where it was lodged for awhile, without participation of its material principle from her." [41] Against the ancient "Marcionites" who held to the belief that Jesus "took only the similitude, resemblance, or appearance of our nature on him, and not the thing itself," [42] Willard emphatically insists that Jesus participated directly and fully in "a true, real, substantial humanity." That means that from the moment of his conception he was "a reasonable creature, consisting of a soul and body."

> Consider him in the [human] nature assumed, and he is a compound, limited, timed being. He is a finite creature, hath a body that is circumscribed, and cannot be every where at once, . . . hath an understanding that is bounded, a will that is subordinated, affections that might be excited or stirred, with joy or grief. He was capable of suffering, and being led to a created happiness, for he went in a path of life.[43]

Willard presses the point that Jesus, more than simply sharing "the same nature" with men, was from "the same original," that he participated in "Adam's family." Therefore "he was flesh of our flesh, and bone of our bone: he had the same blood running in his veins that we have." Because of what he received from the humanity of the Virgin Mary, Jesus was "our brother" who experienced "a fellow feeling" with all other human beings.[44]

Because Jesus stood in Adam's blood-line, he was personally obligated to the terms of the covenant of works just as any other person was. But Jesus was different in one important detail: unlike others, he entered the world sinless. However much Willard cautions against idealizing virginity, he nonetheless believes that Mary was a virgin when

41. CB, p. 298.
42. CB, p. 296.
43. CB, p. 292.
44. CB, pp. 298–300.

she gave birth to Jesus. While she was not herself perfectly pure, her son was "brought into the world with as perfect integrity" as Adam originally had in the Garden of Eden. For Willard that means the "image of God" rested fully upon "the second Adam" from the moment of his conception, and that as he grew up he was filled with "the Spirit"; "he had the habits of knowledge, righteousness and holiness; and he had them beyond measure." [45]

Jesus' real humanity, though, was more than simply filled with the Spirit. Hidden within this humanity was the veiled glory of God, for his human nature did not stand alone by itself but was assumed by "the person of the Son of God." [46] Willard maintains that from the beginning "the individual humanity of Christ" had its "in-being" in the eternal Word:

> It was not first produced and then united to him, but its union was made in the production of it. It was never a tree by itself, but it was at the first inoculated into his divine person and grew upon it. A graft indeed bears other manner of fruit from the stock it is grafted into, and grows upon; but yet it is not a tree by itself; but is a branch in the tree, and a piece of the tree into which it is inserted, having no root or stock but what it receives by this engraftment. The human nature of Christ produceth human actions and effects; but it is sustained, upheld and influenced by the divine person whose it is.[47]

While Jesus had two distinct and irreducible natures, they were united in one person, and that person is divine. Therefore, in dealing with Jesus Christ one stands face to face not with some angel or "third being" [48] but with God himself in his own self-disclosure within the human world.

45. CB, pp. 299–300, 320.
46. CB, p. 293; cf. CR, pp. 59, 84.
47. CB, p. 294.
48. CB, p. 292.

And when Jesus Christ voluntarily laid down his life, "it was God's blood that was shed." [49]

Because Jesus Christ centered his entire being around the glory of God in his "active obedience," and underwent the threatened penalty against sin in his "passive obedience," he fulfilled the conditional terms of the covenant of works and therefore achieved "the reward of life" that Adam forfeited in the Garden of Eden.[50] God did not go back on his pledged word and cancel the covenant of works, for that would have violated the moral government of the universe. God assumed a full human condition and as a "God-man Mediator" satisfied fully the demands of justice agreed upon by Adam and God.

> The covenant of works . . . was not to be taken away by disannulling, but by accomplishment.
>
> . . . that covenant is not removed by rejection, but completion.[51]

The covenant of grace introduced in human history by the Spirit immediately after the fall of "the first Adam" looks forward to and rests upon the completion of the covenant of works by "the second Adam." [52]

Because of who Jesus Christ is, Willard believes that what he does "had a virtue in it that could not be exhausted, being infinite." [53]

> It was an exceeding transcendent price; there is none comparable to it. If all the earth, and seas, and stars too, were massy gold, diamonds and carbuncles, they were of no worth in valuation with this.[54]

49. SM, p. 117; cf. CB, pp. 333–34.
50. LEG, pp. 20–21.
51. CK, pp. 16–17; CB, p. 354; cf. p. 290.
52. CB, pp. 247, 309, 312, 320, 336, 340, 367.
53. CB, p. 253.
54. CB, p. 283.

The "infinite value" Jesus' obedience achieved is so vast, in Willard's opinion, that it could satisfy the requirements of the law for "all the sin of all sinners in the world." [55]

Even though Christ's triumph carries "infinite worth" and the proclamation of God's grace in the new covenant is unlimited, the efficacy of the atonement extends only to those who will drink from the fountain of grace that the resurrection of Jesus Christ opens.[56] Those the Spirit leads into an internal relationship to the new covenant are the ones that Jesus Christ represents as "a public person." [57] "His people" hear in good faith the promise of forgiveness and with good cheer begin now to center their loyalties and loves in God.[58]

The most profound conviction in Willard's "Systematical Divinity" is that no matter how grievously we may have ruptured our relationship to God, we can now begin to "direct all our actions, natural, civil, religious to his glory," [59] because of what was accomplished by Jesus Christ the "God-man Mediator." Here and now the humanity represented in the second Adam enters the kingdom of the God and Father of Jesus Christ.

The eternal covenant of redemption

Willard's route to the ultimate foundation of man's recovery of the fullness of being is contained in the assertion that "it is God that loved us; God that appointed us to the kingdom." [60] Any position, therefore, that permits a

55. TBM, p. 36; cf. FO, p. 29; SM, p. 122; CB, pp. 305, 334, 355, 380; DJ, p. 75.
56. FO, p. 29; cf. BFD, pp. 243–45; MM, p. 388; TBM, p. 257; CR, p. 49.
57. TBM, p. 93; CB, pp. 351–52.
58. CK, p. 96.
59. CB, p. 6.
60. CB, p. 276.

cleavage between God the Father and the Son, by suggesting that forgiving love flows only from Jesus Christ because
the Father "as a provoked judge . . . hates us," is seriously
defective in Willard's eyes.[61] Not only does it vitiate the
unity of divine action; it undercuts utterly the very foundation of man's happiness. That is why Willard puts to
himself this rhetorical question in his *Sacramental Meditations:*

> But shall my thoughts terminate on the person of Christ,
> and limit themselves to the good will of the Son of God in
> this affair? No, no, for though here be enough to swallow
> me up, and loose me in ecstasies, yet I must trace it into the
> boundless ocean of the divine love, where let me be swallowed
> up and never find bank nor bottom.[62]

Structurally Willard insists that the Spirit applies what
the Son achieves, and the Son achieves what the Father
appoints: "In a word, God's election, Christ's redemption, and the Spirit's application carry on the same design;
and consequently have the same subject." [63] This is Willard's reading of the medieval rule that "all the divine
works that are done by God out of himself, are common to
the Trinity." [64]

The mystery of the triune God is not a speculative nicety
in Willard's thought. The doctrine of the Trinity permeates
the fabric of his understanding of man's "restitution" from
beginning to end.

Man in integrity might be happy in the enjoyment of one
God; but fallen man cannot be recovered without a Trinity.[65]

61. SM, p. 127.
62. SM, p. 119.
63. CB, p. 282; cf. p. 427; TBM, p. 93; SM, p. 139; CR, pp. 22, 39.
64. CB, p. 426; cf. CR, pp. 16, 21.
65. CB, p. 100; cf. SM, p. 120.

Because of the soteriological intent of his trinitarian formulation, Willard acknowledges straightforwardly that the triune God cannot be discovered through "the light of nature." "The works of creation and providence declare a God, but not a Trinity." [66] Where God's being and power are refracted through "the glass of creation," and his wisdom and goodness are refracted through "the glass of providence," God's gracious love is refracted in "the glass of the Scriptures," especially in Jesus Christ.[67]

Beginning with the divine love present in Jesus Christ, Willard advances through the analogous "notion of a covenant" to track down "the original . . . wellhead" of the triune God's eternal love.[68]

Back before the world was anything other than an idea in the mind of God, "in that eternity which had no beginning," the Father, the Son, and the Spirit reached an agreement which Willard calls "the covenant of redemption." And in this "firm and inviolable covenant" the Son promises to stand as a "surety" for all those the Father appoints to be vessels of "the glory of his grace." [69] The Father and the Spirit in return promise to restore to active communion those the Son freely represents. According to Willard, this eternal intertrinitarian covenant is the constitutional order that permits "the essential glory" of that love which characterizes God's own "heart" to be reflected in the created world. Or to turn the point around, Willard argues that those who come to be new creatures in Christ through the covenant of grace are a "mirror" in which "the declarative glory" of God's love is visible in human history.[70]

---

66. CB, pp. 97–98.
67. CP, p. 132.
68. SM, p. 121; CR, p. 2; cf. FO, p. 128.
69. CR, p. 38; cf. SM, p. 114; CB, p. 302; TBM, p. 91.
70. CR, p. 70; cf. CB, p. 254.

Because the "God-man Mediator" fulfilled the terms the Son of God agreed to in the eternal covenant of redemption, Willard believes that the Spirit can and does implant the love for God in the hearts and minds of the faithful, and that the Father rejoices in man's homecoming. "His heart therefore as well as his word is in it. And as the Son delighted to do his Father's will, so the Father no less delighted in performing his promise to him." [71] In Willard's considered opinion, an adequately Christian understanding of grace is not reached until one sees that "the heart of the great God is as much engaged in love to poor men that have undone themselves that they may be saved, as the heart of Christ was in going through that great work in which it was accomplished." [72] The "fidelity of God" [73] is Willard's ultimate anchor-point in believing and proclaiming that man's natural desire for an infinite good can be completed in a vision of God, the living God who is Creator, Governor, and Redeemer.

Human happiness and Puritan salvation

In Willard's reading the decisive difference between high paganism and Christianity turns on the latter's belief that man's essential being can be fulfilled and his "pursuit of happiness" satisfied only by the divine love present in supernatural grace. What "heathen moralists" could achieve by only following the light of nature was to suppress the more extravagant pulsations of human sensuality. What they could not do, according to Willard, was to heal "man's condition" from the inside out.[74] Against Stoic suppression,

71. CB, p. 336.
72. DJ, p. 77.
73. CR, p. 156.
74. See above, chap. 7, second and third sections, especially nn. 18, 19, 23.

the most serious alternative to Christianity in the western world since the Roman Empire, Willard celebrates the freedom of the Christian man:

> Stoicism . . . would hamstring nature, and cut off the affections from their natural activity, as if they had been given to and put into men for nothing else but to be suppressed; and to make no use of; as if he could enjoy no benefit by them but only by doing of violence to them: whereas the Word of God and the rules of religion teach us, not to destroy, but to improve every faculty that is in us, and in particular our affections, to the glory of God who gave them to us; and hereby it comes to pass that all in us may be actively engaged in his service. And truly, whatsoever men may think, if God should lose the honor of the employment of our affections for him, we should rob him of a great deal of his due, yea cut off the very feet of our souls, and how then should we be able to run the race of his commandments.[75]

What God is seeking is not the partial response of a man who keeps himself within the limits of legality by "outward restraints." Against this type of "slavish fear" the Spirit is seeking to free the whole man for spontaneous and cheerful enjoyment of the natural moral law of God in and for its own intrinsic goodness.

For quite similar reasons Willard responds negatively to the nightmarish question about whether one should be willing to be damned for the greater glory of God:

> A desire after happiness, and an abhorrence of misery are naturally seated in a man by a concreated principle. Now such principles as God put into man's nature in creation, and stamped indelibly upon his being, not capable of being obliterated, were therefore put in him to be helps to lead him right to his end for which he was made; and therefore to be willing to be damned, is a transgression against the

75. MC, p. 38.

nature of man; it is a violence offered to his own being and inclinations.[76]

The Spirit's activity in applying grace to the human soul does not destroy or violate the natural inclinations of man; throughout the transforming process the Spirit is acting to rectify man's vital center so that his natural desire for happiness will be satisfied.

> Man's great business which he hath in this life to trade for, is happiness. It is that which every man ought to aim at, and is indeed the thing which all the children of men do propound to themselves. . . . They differ indeed in the ways and means (and there are almost as many courses taken to obtain it as there are men that seek it) yet all naturally agree in this one end, viz. that they may do and be well. And the right improving of suitable means to this end, is the great thing wherein man's wisdom doth most properly consist.

> As happiness is our subjective, so is the glory of God our objective end; and God hath tied these together so inseparably, that men cannot possibly make a separation of them, without his unspeakable loss.[77]

What hold these subjective and objective ends together in Willard's "Systematical Divinity" is the triumph of grace accomplished by Jesus Christ, the God-man Mediator of the new covenant.

76. MM, pp. 249–50.
77. MM, pp. 66–67.

Epilogue

Every one is ready to make his remarks on the time that he lives in and which pass over him, and to judge of them whether the days are good or evil. The generality of men take their measures from the observation of outward providence: if there be outward peace and plenty, they call them happy days; if outward distress and trouble, they call them evil. But we have a better rule, and more safe for Christians, and that is to judge according as this fountain is opened amongst us. The more of Christ that a people enjoy, the happier are they, and the less he is known and acknowledged in his great design of mediatorship, the greater is the infelicity of such a people; and by this rule I believe the times are evil in the most places that are called Christian; inasmuch as it is a day wherein the greatest number of those that should preach the doctrines of Christ, of redemption, justification, sanctification, and eternal life to be obtained by him, and so to be the instruments of opening the fountain to men; do rather endeavor to obscure them, by perverting the great doctrine of justification by his righteousness alone, and confounding new covenant obedience with mere morality, or a legal righteousness. How contrary are these things to those which will be the glory of the times of refreshment.[1]

1. FO, pp. 123–24.

Shortly before his death Samuel Willard baptized Benjamin Franklin (1706–90), who more than perhaps any other eighteenth-century American epitomized the Enlightenment in the New World. In one much quoted passage from his *Autobiography,* Franklin discloses the continuities and discontinuities between his Puritan background and his own philosophy of life:

> I had been religiously educated as a Presbyterian; and though some of the dogmas of the persuasion, such as the eternal decrees of God, election, reprobation, etc., appeared to me unintelligible, others doubtful, and I early absented myself from the public assemblies of the sect, Sunday being my studying-day, I never was without some religious principles. I never doubted, for instance, the existence of the Deity, that he made the world and governed it by his providence, that the most acceptable service of God was the doing good to man, that our souls are immortal, and that all crime will be punished and virtue rewarded either here or hereafter. These I esteemed the essentials of every religion, and being to be found in all the religions we had in our country, I respected them all, though with different degrees of respect as I found them more or less mixed with other articles which without any tendency to inspire, promote, or confirm morality, served principally to divide us and make us unfriendly to one another.[2]

While Franklin's distaste for dogmatic beliefs in this and numerous other passages is obvious, his emphasis upon "morality" and "religious principles" is conspicuously present, too. The metaphysical and moral tenets mentioned here, furthermore, are not significantly different from those expounded above in the chapters on "God the Master Workman," "The Created and Governed World," "Man

2. L. Jesse Lemisch, *Benjamin Franklin: The Autobiography and Other Writings* (New York, 1961), pp. 92–93.

the Reasonable Creature," and "The Natural Moral Law."
This same general point could be made by comparing Willard's natural theology with the chapters on "The Supreme
Workman" and "The Physiology of Thought and Morals"
in Daniel J. Boorstin's seminal study, *The Lost World of
Thomas Jefferson*.³ One way of interpreting the Enlightenment in America is to see it in direct continuity with those
parts of Puritan Divinity which are under the determination of "right reason" operating with "the light of nature"
alone. From Willard's natural theology to Franklin's deistic
position it is a small step indeed. And it is precisely because of continuity on this level that David Levin can make
a good case for reading Franklin as *The Puritan in the
Enlightenment*.⁴

The discontinuities between Willard and Franklin,
however, are massive and decisive. Their differences turn
on the question, "is natural theology sufficient for salvation?" That question appeared on the broadsides distributed
at Harvard commencements in 1674, 1701 and 1704, and
Willard was the acting president on the last two occasions.⁵ On all three the respondents were announced as
answering negatively. If pressed, Franklin would have answered affirmatively; or perhaps more modestly, that it was
a sufficient guide for life, liberty, and the pursuit of happiness in colonial America.

Willard realized that New England was caught up in a
profound transition that engulfed a considerable part of
Western Christendom during his lifetime, a turning of the

3. loc. cit. (Boston, 1948).
4. David Levin, ed., *The Puritan in the Enlightenment: Franklin
Edwards* (Chicago, 1963). For a thorough discussion of Franklin's religious views see Alfred Owen Aldridge, *Benjamin Franklin and Nature's God* (Durham, N.C., 1967).
5. Samuel Eliot Morison, *Harvard College in the Seventeenth Century* (Cambridge, Mass., 1936), pp. 606, 632, 634.

human spirit that Paul Hazard has called *La Crise de la Conscience Européenne.*[6] The crisis arose, according to Willard, from a shift in the spiritual and intellectual life of the cultural elite, for "the pretended moralists of the age we live in . . . level all moral duties to man's power" and tacitly ignore the grace of God. In Willard's eyes not immorality, but "mere morality," was crushing the human spirit. What was troubling Willard most was not unseemly disorder or wanton sensuality, but the fact that in New England "forwardness and zeal for God is almost out of date" and "lukewarm-confession is much in credit, being very fashionable." [7] That is why in *Morality not to be relied on for Life* he issued this solemn warning to the clergy:

> Hence what caution had gospel ministers need to use in their preaching up of moral duties? That it is their duty to preach them, and press them upon their hearers is certain, otherwise they cannot be faithful in declaring the whole counsel of God. And yet if they so preach them as to revive the covenant of works, to advance the righteousness of man, and depreciate the righteousness of Christ, they are far from being the ministers of Christ, and are indeed the very betrayers of souls to destruction, as far as in them lieth. Nor indeed do I know of any thing which doth more threaten the undermining of true Christianity, and the bringing in of another gospel, than the putting of moral virtues into a legal dress, and without any more ado to commend them to us as the graces of our Christian religion. He who when he hath told men all the moral duties required in the law of God, and laid them out according to the nature of them, as they were enjoined on them in the first covenant, saith to them, this do and live, and doth not endeavor to show them that there is something more wanting, without which

6. The American edition is Paul Hazard, *The European Mind: 1680–1715* (New York, 1963; the original French edition, 1935).
7. CK, p. 106; CB, p. 581.

they are undone, will be found an enemy of grace and a murderer of souls.[8]

Within the framework of Willard's perceptions and evaluations, the Age of Reason represented the triumph of "mere morality, or a legal righteousness" over the conditions of the new covenant. Instead of receiving in good faith a new supernatural principle to re-create the inner man and reorient the whole man towards his proper end, the "moralists" of the Enlightenment were satisfied with the laws of nature and nature's God.

Squarely within a climate of opinion that was running against the spirituality of the Puritan faith, Willard did more than lament the declension of piety and the rise of moralism.[9] He spoke for God's kingdom and believed passionately that God was about to do a new work.

We are some of us going off the stage, and are very solicitous about what shall become of ours when we are gone. There are many saddening considerations that appear in our view, which do sometimes fill us with perplexity; but let such as fear God look through and beyond the present discouragements; and we leave our children to a good God, a covenant keeping God, whose truth and faithfulness we may safely rely upon; but it is comfort for us to think that that day is not far off; and though we may not live to see the dawnings of it, yet our posterity may see the breaking of it, and partake in the happy benefits that it shall bring to the church of God.[10]

While "there are many saddening considerations that appear in our view," God's arm is not shortened; therefore,

---

8. MRL, pp. 26–27.

9. See Joseph Haroutunian, *Piety versus Moralism: The Passing of the New England Theology* (New York, 1932); aand Sydney E. Ahlstrom, "The Saybrook Platform: A 250th Anniversary Retrospect," *Bulletin of the Congregational Library* (Oct., 1959), 2: 1, 5–10.

10. FO, pp. 126–27.

Let us not be over anxious for the church. Let us not torment our minds with sinking thoughts about it. To be solicitous for the cause and people of God, and duly affected with the troubles that are brought upon them in a dark time, becometh all those who love Zion. . . . But we are too prone to sink in our spirits, and to give up all for gone, when we see clouds gathering, and a storm impending, but this posture very ill becomes those that are true believers. Let us then always bear in our thoughts, with a firm credit, that God knows intimately what is now in doing; and is not forgetful of his people whom he hath loved. Let us not then be afraid, or discouraged, but pursue our duty, and wait in hope.[11]

Willard's "hope" centered on his conviction that the millennium would shortly come and "God will bring his church out of darkness, into light, and take them out of the horrible pit, and set their feet upon the rock." On how long this coming age would last, Willard was less than certain, though on one occasion at least he did say, "if it be allowed to be a full thousand years, I see no Scripture argument against it." Much more important, though, was the claim that "there shall be a very considerable time of tranquillity afforded to the church, after her coming out of the wilderness." [12]

What Willard anticipated for this coming period of "outward tranquillity" was an age in which the people of God would be permitted to extend without hindrance the means of grace throughout the world, an age of the Spirit in which the minds and hearts of men would be more powerfully moved to celebrate the goodness of being and the glory of God in all things.

There shall be more of it [that is, light in the future] than hath been, ever since the apostle's time; and possibly, as

11. CSGC, pp. 46–47.
12. FO, pp. 126–27; CSGC, pp. 51–55.

to the generality of Christians more than we discovered to
them in those times. There will be a clearer dispensation
of the truths of the Word of God, and a more distinct discovery of the mind of God therein, than in the ages going
before.[13]

In the technical language of theology Willard was a "post-
millennialist," that is, one who expects the millennium to
occur prior to the return of Christ in glory. What this
means in terms of Willard's stance towards the future is
that he thought history would improve before the final
consummation.

While Willard never wrote anything analogous to Jonathan Edwards' *History of the Work of Redemption*, the
pivotal points in Willard's reading of the history of the
divine-human community are readily discernible, for the
broad sweep of history passes through four distinct stages.
First, before the fall of Adam, the covenant of works alone
defined the constitutional order of the life-relationship
between man and God. Second, from the initial promise to
fallen Adam to the incarnation of Jesus, the covenant of
grace was extended to the church of the Old Testament
(Israel). Third, from the time of Jesus to the end of history,
the new covenant is intended for the whole world. Within
this "evangelical dispensation of the kingdom of Christ,"
moreover, is a fourth period, the coming "times of refreshment" when there will be a relative improvement in "the
privileges of the church, both spiritual and temporal."

In the millennium to come, it should be emphasized,
Willard believed that there would be only "a fullness not
of absolute, but comparative perfection." [14] Absolute perfection is reserved for the transhistorical state of "glory."
In this world ambiguity will always mark the church's life.

13. CB, p. 249.
14. FO, p. 118.

To expect an age in which "there shall be neither ignorance, nor error, nor trouble upon the professing people of God is but a dream; and those who feed themselves up with such a hope, do but feed on ashes." The church is never triumphant in this world. Militant it remains all the way to the end of history in a "checkered state," a tissue of light and darkness, good and evil, faith and unfaith. Nonetheless, Willard believed "that there are better times coming on." [15] When the Great Awakening erupted along the Atlantic seaboard during the 1730's, it is not surprising that many understood it as the coming of the Age of the Spirit.[16]

Both the Age of Reason and the Age of the Spirit, both the Enlightenment and the Awakening, both Benjamin Franklin and Jonathan Edwards have deep but different roots in the Puritan synthesis. And from Samuel Willard's "Systematical Divinity" the lines flowed forward through each into the life of the mind in America.

15. FO, p. 127.
16. See C. H. Maxson, *The Great Awakening in the Middle Colonies* (Chicago, 1920); E. S. Gaustad, *The Great Awakening in New England* (New York, 1957); Alan Heimert, *Religion and the American Mind: From the Great Awakening to the Revolution* (Cambridge, Mass., 1966).

Bibliographical Essay

Because comprehensive bibliographies on seventeenth-century New England are readily available in the Harper Torchbooks edition of *The Puritans: A Sourcebook of Their Writings,* edited by Perry Miller and Thomas H. Johnson (New York, 1963), this essay will be only a brief guide to the most helpful secondary literature informing this study. A full listing of Willard's publications is given at the end.

While a fantastic array of books could be cited as contributory to an understanding of Willard's theology, these first rate interpretations will suffice for an introduction to the resources within the heritage Willard received from Europe:

F. C. Copleston, *A History of Philosophy,* Volume 2 (Westminster, Md., 1960)

John Burnaby, *Amor Dei: A Study of the Religion of St. Augustine* (London, 1938)

Etienne Gilson, *Elements of Christian Philosophy,* on Thomas Aquinas (New York, 1960)

Heiko Augustinus Oberman, *The Harvest of Medieval Theology: Gabriel Biel and Late Medieval Nominalism* (Cambridge, Mass., 1963)

Gordon Rupp, *The Righteousness of God: Luther Studies* (London, 1953)

Francois Wendel, *Calvin: The Origins and Development of His Religious Thought* (New York, 1963; original French, 1950)

Robert P. Scharlemann, *Thomas Aquinas and John Gerhard* (New Haven, Conn., 1964)

For convenient sourcebooks on the immediate theological context in which Willard worked, see:

John D. Eusden, ed., *The Marrow of Theology: William Ames, 1576–1633* (Boston, 1968)
John W. Beardslee, III, ed., *Reformed Dogmatics: J. Wollebius, G. Voetius, F. Turretin* (New York, 1965)
Heinrich Heppe, *Reformed Dogmatics Set Out and Illustrated from the Sources,* transl. by G. T. Thomson (London, 1950)

No student of Puritanism in New England could possibly express his appreciation adequately for the pioneering and thought-provoking studies by Perry Miller:

Errand into the Wilderness (Cambridge, Mass., 1956), especially, "The Marrow of Puritan Divinity"
The New England Mind: The Seventeenth Century (Cambridge, Mass., 1954)
Orthodoxy in Massachusetts: 1630–1650 (Boston, 1933)
The New England Mind: From Colony to Province (Cambridge, Mass., 1953)

Kenneth B. Murdock's *Literature & Theology in Colonial New England* (Cambridge, Mass., 1949) still provides insights into the workings of the Puritan mind, as does Samuel Eliot Morison's *The Intellectual Life of Colonial New England* (Ithaca, N.Y., 1956, originally published as *The Puritan Pronaos* in 1936). Morison's *The Founding of Harvard College* and *Harvard College in the Seventeenth Century* (Cambridge, Mass., 1936) are beautifully executed histories, but they are weakest precisely in the philosophical and theological areas.

On particular topics that cut across the substantive chapters of this study, these works were indispensable:

Edmund S. Morgan, *Visible Saints: The History of a Puritan Idea* (New York, 1963)
Edmund S. Morgan, *Roger Williams: The Church and the State* (New York, 1967)

Norman Pettit, *The Heart Prepared: Grace and Conversion in Puritan Spiritual Life* (New Haven, Conn., 1966)

Alan Ludwig, *Graven Images* (Middletown, Conn., 1966)

In preparing the biographical section, several biographies were useful:

Seymour Van Dyken, *Samuel Willard, 1640–1707: Preacher of Orthodoxy in an Era of Change* (Grand Rapids, Mich., 1972)

Kenneth Ballard Murdock, *Increase Mather, The Foremost American Puritan* (Cambridge, Mass., 1925)

Ola Elizabeth Winslow, *Samuel Sewall of Boston* (New York, 1964)

And the documents gathered by Samuel A. Green, M.D., and H. A. Hill are critically important:

Samuel A. Green, ed., *The Early Records of Groton, Massachusetts* (Groton, Mass., 1880)

Samuel A. Green, *Groton During the Indian Wars* (Groton, Mass., 1883)

Samuel A. Green, *Groton in the Witchcraft Times* (Groton, Mass., 1883)

H. A. Hill, *History of the Old South Church* (Boston, 1890)

For the climate of opinion around the turn of the century, Paul Hazard's *The European Mind: 1680–1715* (New York, 1963; original French, 1935) provides an overview of the continental cultural situation. C. R. Cragg, *From Puritanism to the Age of Reason* (Cambridge, 1950) is a valuable treatment of the English religious scene during Willard's lifetime. Sydney E. Ahlstrom, "The Saybrook Platform: A 250th Anniversary Retrospect," *Bulletin of the Congregational Library* (Oct., 1959) covers in brief compass the turn of the century in New England.

The best introductions to the Great Awakening are C. H. Maxson, *The Great Awakening in the Middle Colonies* (Chicago, 1920), and E. S. Gaustad, *The Great Awakening in New England* (New York, 1957).

Religious thought in the eighteenth-century colonies has received sustained attention. The more useful books for understanding the age after Willard are:

Joseph Haroutunian, *Piety versus Moralism: The Passing of the New England Theology* (New York, 1932)

Alan Heimert, *Religion and the American Mind: From the Great Awakening to the Revolution* (Cambridge, Mass., 1966)

Conrad Wright, *The Beginnings of Unitarianism in America* (Boston, 1955)

Alfred Owen Aldridge, *Benjamin Franklin and Nature's God* (Durham, N.C., 1967)

Daniel J. Boorstin, *The Lost World of Thomas Jefferson* (Boston, 1948)

The way religious beliefs shaped the mentality of the early national period is told with admirable skill in the book Perry Miller was writing when he died, *The Life of the Mind in America: From the Revolution to the Civil War* (New York, 1965).

Publications by Samuel Willard

This section is arranged alphabetically according to the initials of the short titles given in the body of this study. The short title follows, and then the full original title. Evans Microtext numbers are added.

BDYS   *Brief Directions to a Young Scholar.*
            Brief Directions to a Young Scholar Designing the Ministry, for the Study of Divinity. Boston: J. Draper, 1735. Edited by Joseph Sewall and Thomas Prince, Evans 3976, 7 pp.

BFD   *Barren Figtree's Doom.*
            The Barren Figtree's Doom: or A brief discourse wherein is set forth the woful danger of all who abide unfruitful under Gospel-priviledges, and God's husbandry. Being the substance of sixteen sermons preached on Christ's parable of the figtree. Boston: Benjamin Harris, John Allen, 1691. Evans 581, 300 pp.

BL   *Brotherly Love.*
            Brotherly Love Described and Directed: As it was casuistically handled in two sermons preached on the lecture in Boston. Boston, 1701. Published with *Christian's Exercise*, Evans 1033, 51 pp.

BP   *Best Priviledge.*
            The Best Priviledge: or A sermon wherein the great advantage of enjoying the oracles of God is displayed, and the duty of such as have them is urged. Preached

on the lecture in Boston on June *19, 1701.* Boston:
Printed by B. Green and J. Allen, 1701. Evans 1031,
30 pp.

BRGK   *Brief Reply to Mr. George Keith.*
A Brief Reply to Mr. George Keith: In answer to a
script of his, entitled "A Refutation of a Dangerous
and Hurtfull Opinion, Maintained by Mr. Samuel
Willard." Boston, 1703. Evans 1150, 60 pp.

CB   *Compleat Body.*
A Compleat Body of Divinity in Two Hundred and
Fifty Expository Lectures on the Assembly's Shorter
Catechism: Wherein the doctrines of the Christian
religion are unfolded, their truth confirmed, their ex-
cellence displayed, their usefulness improved, contrary
errors and vices refuted and exposed, objections an-
swered, controversies settled, cases of conscience re-
solved, and a great light thereby reflected on the
present age. Boston: B. Green and S. Kneeland, 1726.
Edited by Joseph Sewall and Thomas Prince, Evans,

CE   2828, 999 pp. *Christian's Exercise.*
The Christian's Exercise by Satan's Temptation: or
An essay to discover the methods which this adversary
useth to tempt the children of God, and to direct
them how to escape the mischief thereof. Being the
substance of several sermons preached on that sub-
ject. Boston: B. Green and J. Allen, 1701. Evans 1033,
216 pp.

CGR   *Character of a Good Ruler.*
The Character of a Good Ruler: As it was recom-
mended in a sermon preached before his Excellency
the Governour and the Honourable Counsellors and
the Assembly of the Representatives of the province
of Massachusetts-Bay in New-England on May 30,
1694, which was the day for election of Counsellors
for that province. Boston: Benjamin Harris, 1694.
Evans 711, 31 pp.

CK   *Covenant Keeping.*
Covenant-Keeping, the Way to Blessedness: or A

brief discourse wherein is shewn the connexion which there is between the promise, on God's part, and duty, on our part, in the Covenant of Grace, as it was delivered in several sermons, preached in order to solemn renewing of covenant. Boston: James Glen, 1682. Evans 335, 128 pp.

CP   *Child's Portion.*
The Child's Portion: or The unseen glory of the children of God, asserted, and proved: together with several other sermons occasionally preached, and now published. Boston: Samuel Green, 1684. Evans 380, 144 pp.

CR   *Covenant of Redemption.*
The Doctrine of the Covenant of Redemption: Wherein is laid the foundation of all our hopes and happiness. Briefly opened and improved. Boston: Benjamin Harris, 1693. Evans 684, 165 pp.

CSGC   *Checkered State of the Gospel Church.*
The Checkered State of the Gospel Church: Being the substance of a sermon prepared for, and in part preached on September 18, 1701. Being a day of publick fasting and prayer. Boston: B. Green and J. Allen, 1701. Evans 1032, 64 pp.

DJ   *Discourse of Justification.*
A Brief Discourse of Justification: Wherein the doctrine is plainly laid down according to the Scriptures. As it was delivered in several sermons on this subject. Boston: S[amuel] G[reen], 1686. Evans 423, 168 pp.

DP   *Duty of a People.*
The Duty of a People that have Renewed their Covenant with God: Opened and urged in a sermon preached to the second church in Boston in New-England, March 17, 1679/80 after that church had explicitly and most solemnly renewed the ingagement of themselves to God, and one to another. Boston: John Foster, 1680. Evans 296, 13 pp.

DTGNV   *Danger of Taking God's Name in Vain.*
The Danger of Taking God's Name in Vain: As it

was delivered in a sermon. Boston: Benjamin Harris
and John Allen, 1691. Evans 582, 30 pp.

EP   *Evangelical Perfection.*
*Evangelical Perfection: or How far the Gospel re-
quires believers to aspire after being completely per-
fect. As it was delivered on a lecture at Boston on
June 10, 1694.* Published with *Fountain Opened,*
Evans 960, 41 pp.

FO   *Fountain Opened.*
*The Fountain Opened: or The great Gospel priviledge
of having Christ exhibited to sinfull men. Wherein
also is proved that there shall be a national calling
of the Jews, from Zech. 13. 1.* Boston: B. Green and
J. Allen, 1700. Evans 960, 166 pp.; reprinted in 1722
and 1727.

FofO   *Fear of an Oath.*
*The Fear of an Oath: or Some cautions to be used
about swearing, if we would approve our selves truly
Godly, as it was discoursed in a sermon, preached at
Boston, on the lecture, January 30, 1700, 1.* Boston,
1701. Evans 1034, 29 pp.

FTST   *Fiery Tryal No Strange Thing.*
*The Fiery Tryal No Strange Thing: Delivered in a
sermon preached at Charlestown, February 15, 1681.
Being a day of humiliation.* Boston, 1682. Evans 336,
19 pp.

HE   *High Esteem.*
*The High Esteem Which God Hath of the Death of
His Saints: As it was delivered in a sermon preached
October 7, 1683. Occasioned by the death of the
Worshipful John Hull, Esq., who deceased October 1,
1683.* Boston: Samuel Green, 1683. Evans 356, 18 pp.

HG   *Heart Garrisoned.*
*The Heart Garrisoned: or The wisdome, and care of
the spiritual souldier above all things to safeguard
his heart. Delivered in a sermon which was preached
to the honoured gentlemen of the artillery company,
on the day of their election, Boston in New-England,*

June 5, 1676. Cambridge: Samuel Green, 1676. Evans 227, 21 pp.

HM   *Heavenly Merchandize.*

Heavenly Merchandize: or The purchasing of truth recommended and the selling of it disswaded; as it was delivered in several sermons upon Prov. 23. 23. Boston: Samuel Green, 1686. Evans 424, 171 pp.

IS   *Impenitent Sinners.*

Impenitent Sinners Warned of Their Misery and Summoned to Judgment: Delivered in two sermons, the former on the Sabbath, November 6, the other on the lecture following, November 10, 1698. Occasioned by the amazing instance of a miserable creature, who stood condemned for murdering her infant begotten in whoredom. To which are subjoyned the solemn words spoken to her, on those opportunities. Published for the warning of others. Boston: B. Green and J. Allen, 1698. Evans 856, 52 pp.

ITS   *Israel's True Safety.*

Israel's True Safety: Offered in a sermon, before his Excellency, the Honourable Council, and Representatives of the province of the Massachusetts-Bay in New-England on March 15, 1704. Being a day set apart for solemn fasting and prayer. Boston: B. Green, 1704. Evans 1198, 34 pp.

JMP   *Just Man's Prerogative.*

The Just Man's Prerogative: A sermon preached privately, September 27, 1706. On the solemn occasion for the consolation of a sorrowful family mourning over the immature death of a pious son, viz. Mr. Simeon Stoddard, who was found barbarously murdered in Chelsea-Fields near London, May 14, 1706. Boston: B. Green, 1706. Evans 1286, 28 pp.

LEG   *Law Established by the Gospel.*

The Law Established by the Gospel: or A brief discourse wherein is asserted and declared the great honour which is put upon the law of God in the Gospel way of justification by faith alone. Being the substance of a sermon preached on the lecture in Boston, September 20, 1694. Boston: Bartholomew Green, 1694. Evans 712, 39 pp.

LHB   *Laying the Hand on the Bible.*
A Brief Discourse Concerning That Ceremony of Laying the Hand on the Bible in Swearing. London: J. Z., 1689. 8 pp.

LP   *Love's Pedigree.*
Love's Pedigree: or A discourse shewing the grace of love in a believer to be of a divine original. Delivered in a sermon preached at the lecture in Boston, February 29, 1699/1700. Boston: B. Green and J. Allen, 1700. Evans 961, 28 pp.

MC   *Mourner's Cordial.*
The Mourner's Cordial Against Excessive Sorrow Discovering What Grounds of Hope God's People Have Concerning Their Dead Friends. Boston: Benjamin Harris and John Allen, 1691. Evans 583, 137 pp.

MM   *Mercy Magnified.*
Mercy Magnified on a Penitent Prodigal: or A brief discourse, wherein Christ's parable of the lost son found is opened and applied, as it was delivered in sundry sermons. Boston: Samuel Green, 1684. Evans 379, 391 pp.

MRL   *Morality not to be Relied on for Life.*
Morality not to be Relied on for Life: or A brief discourse, discovering the one thing wanting, which leaves the legalist short of life eternal. Delivered in a sermon on the lecture in Boston, May 23, 1700. Boston: B. Green and J. Allen, 1700. Evans 962, 28 pp.

MW   *Man of War.*
The Man of War: A sermon preached to the artillery company at Boston on June 5, 1699. Being the anniversary day for their election of officers. Boston: B. Green and J. Allen, 1699. Evans 900, 30 pp.

NS   *Necessity of Sincerity.*
The Necessity of Sincerity in Renewing Covenant:

Opened and urged in a sermon preached to the third gathered church in Boston, New-England, June 29, 1680, on the day wherein they solemnly renewed covenant. Boston: James Glen, 1682. Evans 335, 18 pp.

PGP *All Plots Against God and His People.*

All Plots Against God and His People Detected and Defeated: As it was delivered in a sermon at a fast kept by the first gathered church in Boston, January 25, 1682. Published with *Child's Portion*, Evans 380, 28 pp.

PIC *Prognostics of Impending Calamities.*

Prognostics of Impending Calamities: Delivered in a sermon preached on the lecture at Boston, July 17, 1701. Occasioned by the death of the Truly Honourable William Stoughton, Esq., Lieutenant Governour, and of the province of the Massachusetts Bay, in New England. Boston: B. Green and J. Allen, 1701. Evans 1035, 32 pp.

PK *Promise Keeping.*

Promise-Keeping a Great Duty: As it was delivered in a sermon. Boston: Benjamin Harris and John Allen, 1691. Evans 584, 28 pp.

PPRM *Principles of the Protestant Religion Maintained.*

The Principles of the Protestant Religion Maintained: And churches of New-England, in the profession and exercise thereof defended against all the calumnies of one George Keith, a Quaker, in a book lately published, Pensilvania, to undermine them both. By the ministers of the Gospel in Boston. Boston: Printed by Richard Pierce, 1690. The Preface is signed by James Allen, Joshua Moodey, Samuel Willard, and Cotton Mather. Evans 502, 156 pp.

PT *Peril of the Times.*

The Peril of the Times Displayed: or The danger of men's taking up with a form of Godliness, but denying the power of it. Being the substance of several sermons preached. Boston: B. Green and J. Allen, 1700. Evans 963, 168 pp.

RAD   *Remedy Against Despair.*
               *A Remedy Against Despair: or Brief discourse wherein
               great sinners are encouraged and directed how to
               improve the consideration of the greatness of their
               sins in praying to God for pardon. Being the sub-
               stance of two sermons preached at the lecture in
               Boston, 1699.* Boston: B. Green and J. Allen, 1700.
               Evans 964, 70 pp.

RDPT   *Rules for the Discerning of the Present Times. Rules
               for the Discerning of the Present Times: Recom-
               mended to the people of God in New-England in a
               sermon preached on the lecture in Boston, November
               27, 1692.* Boston: Benjamin Harris, 1693. Evans 685,
               30 pp.

RGD   *Reformation the Great Duty.*
               *Reformation the Great Duty of an Afflicted People:
               Setting forth the sin and danger there is in neglecting
               of it, under the continued and repeated judgments
               of God. Being the substance of what was preached
               on a solemn day of humiliation kept by the third
               gathered church in Boston on August 23, 1694.* Bos-
               ton: Bartholomew Green, 1694. Evans 713, 76 pp.

RMD   *Righteous Man's Death.*
               *The Righteous Man's Death, a Presage of Evil Ap-
               proaching: A sermon occasioned by the death of
               Major Thomas Savage, Esq. Preached February 19,
               1681.* Boston: Samuel Green, 1684. Published with
               Child's Portion, Evans 380, 18 pp.

SD   *Spiritual Desertions.*
               *Spiritual Desertions Discovered and Remedied: Being
               the substance of divers sermons preached for the help
               of dark souls labouring under divine withdrawings.*
               Boston: B. Green and J. Allen, 1699. Evans 901,
               144 pp.

SM   *Sacramental Meditations.*
               *Some Brief Sacramental Meditations Preparatory for
               Communion at the Great Ordinance of the Supper.*
               Boston: B. Green, 1711. Evans 1537, 257 pp.

SMOW   *Some Miscellany Observations on Witchcrafts. Some Miscellany Observations on our Present Debates Respecting Witchcrafts, in a dialogue between S. and B.* Philadelphia: William Bradford, 1692. Republished in 1869, 15 pp.

SPE   *Sermon Preached upon Ezek. 22.* *A Sermon Preached upon Ezek. 22. 30. 31: Occasioned by the death of the much honoured John Leveret, Esq., Governour of the colony of the Massachusetts, N-E.* Boston: John Foster, 1679. Evans 277, 13 pp.

SUC   *Ne Sutor ultra Crepidam.* *Ne Sutor ultra Crepidam: or Brief animadversions upon the New-England Anabaptist late fallacious narrative, wherein the notorious mistakes and falshoods by them published are detected.* Boston: S. Green, 1681. Evans 309, 27 pp.

SWGMI   *Sinfulness of Worshipping God with Men's Institutions. The Sinfulness of Worshipping God with Men's Institutions: As it was delivered in a sermon.* Boston: Benjamin Harris and John Allen, 1691. Evans 585, 29 pp.

TBM   *Truly Blessed Man.* *The Truly Blessed Man: or The way to be happy here and for ever. Being the substance of divers sermons preached on Psalm 32.* Boston: B. Green and J. Allen, 1700. Evans 965, 652 pp.

TS   *Thanksgiving Sermon.* *A Thanksgiving Sermon Preach'd at Boston in New-England, December, 1705, on the Return of a Gentleman from his Travels.* London, 1709, 12 pp.

UI   *Useful Instructions.* *Useful Instructions for a Professing People in Time of Great Security and Degeneracy: Delivered in several sermons on solemn occasions.* Cambridge: Samuel Green, 1673. Not listed in Evans, 80 pp.

WG   *Walking with God.* *Walking with God, the Great Duty and Priviledge of True Christians: In two sermons, preached on the* lecture in the year 1700. Boston: B. Green and J. Allen, 1701. Evans 1036, 56 pp.

WPTC   *Only Sure Way to Prevent Threatned Calamity.*
The Only Sure Way to Prevent Threatned Calamity:
As it was delivered in a sermon preached at the Court
of Election, May 24, 1682. Boston, 1682. Published
with *Child's Portion,* Evans 380, 34 pp.

Index